FUNDAMENTALS OF
Library Instruction

D0083592

ALA FUNDAMENTALS SERIES

FUNDAMENTALS OF
Library Instruction

MONTY L. McADOO

ALA FUNDAMENTALS SERIES

American Library Association : Chicago 2012

Monty L. McAdoo is research and instruction librarian of the Baron-Forness Library at Edinboro University of Pennsylvania. His research interests include faculty understanding and use of information literacy and information technology. McAdoo earned his master's degree in library science at the University of Pittsburgh and his doctorate of education in administration and leadership studies at Indiana University of Pennsylvania.

Printed in the United States of America
16 15 14 13 12   5 4 3 2 1

Extensive effort has gone into ensuring the reliability of the information in this book; however, the publisher makes no warranty, express or implied, with respect to the material contained herein.

ISBNs: 978-0-8389-1141-9 (paper); 978-0-8389-9415-3 (PDF); 978-0-8389-9414-6 (ePub); 978-0-8389-9416-0 (Mobipocket); 978-0-8389-9417-7 (Kindle). For more information on digital formats, visit the ALA Store at alastore.ala.org and select eEditions.

Library of Congress Cataloging-in-Publication Data
McAdoo, Monty L.
  Fundamentals of library instruction / Monty L. McAdoo.
    pages   cm. — (ALA fundamentals series)
  Includes bibliographical references and index.
  ISBN 978-0-8389-1141-9
  1. Library orientation. 2. Library orientation for college students. I. Title.
  Z711.2M33 2012
  025.5'677—dc23
                                                                2011043250

Book design in Museo Sans and Electra by Casey Bayer.
Cover image © Lee Morris/Shutterstock Inc.

⊗ This paper meets the requirements of ANSI/NISO Z39.48–1992 (Permanence of Paper).

ALA Editions purchases fund advocacy, awareness, and accreditation programs for library professionals worldwide.

to Carson . . . my son and greatest teacher

CONTENTS

PREFACE

THE INFORMATION AGE, or "knowledge society," is generally seen as having begun sometime during the last decade or so of the twentieth century. This new age differs in several dramatic ways from its predecessor, the industrial age. Among others, rather than a focus on physical labor and natural resources, for example, the emphasis of the information age is on innovation, knowledge, skills, and ideas. Direct outgrowths include a shift in emphasis from physical assets to intellectual ones and in teachers being seen as facilitators of learning more than "mere" providers of information.

With that mind, it is not surprising that public schools and, more recently, colleges and universities are under increasing pressure to provide practical knowledge and vocational skills needed by today's worker to navigate this evolutionary shift to a "knowledge economy" successfully. In particular, teachers at all levels are being asked more and more to provide opportunities for students to acquire and use "information skills." This is perhaps best reflected in an ever-growing number of accreditation requirements and institutional documents (e.g., mission statements, general education requirements) that make reference to or have specific expectations for things such as "technology competency" and "information literacy" being incorporated into the curriculum.

Libraries and librarians are increasingly being looked to for leadership in this trend. Librarians have long been involved with the educational process, particularly with respect to research and information skills. In fact, it can be argued that, in one form or another, library instruction has been around for as long as there have been libraries. Only recently, however, has that instruction itself become a high-profile item on the agenda of many libraries or librarians.

There are many reasons why instruction has not always been a priority. Among these, the traditional character of librarian education and training is certainly central. Simply put, despite growing demands for instruction, library science programs with an instruction track are virtually nonexistent. Worse, many programs do not have even a single course dealing with instruction in the library context. As a result, the only exposure and "training" that many instruction librarians ever receive is on the job.

Either because of or in spite of this, resources about library instruction are noticeably limited as well. Those resources that are available typically focus on how-to sorts of things, providing specific activities or exercises that can be embedded in a class or program or instructions for how to teach specific things (e.g., subject searching). Few focus on planning instruction, pedagogy, and similar topics surrounding instruction. Those that do often presuppose experience with instruction or a familiarity with instructional design. Others are written from a teacher's perspective, not a librarian's, and thus often lack meaningful context.

Fundamentals of Library Instruction is an attempt to fill this gap in the literature. Instruction is becoming a core responsibility for a growing number of librarians. Unfortunately, many of those who are assigned to teach lack experience doing so. Others want to teach but are not exactly sure how to find the opportunity or what it involves. For others, instruction is simply not their primary area of responsibility. Being about the fundamentals, this book is geared primarily toward these individuals. That said, the book also serves as a helpful set of reminders to even the most experienced of instructors. Despite a bias toward academic librarians and one-shot instruction sessions, the general nature of the book should be valuable to any librarian providing instruction—public, school, or otherwise.

Be aware, this book is in no way intended to be a comprehensive, exhaustive exploration of library instruction. Rather, it is a primer, exploring key topics, issues, and concerns to give a broad overview of all aspects of the instruction process. It also offers suggestions for overcoming challenges and otherwise making instruction and instructors more effective.

After a brief historical overview of instruction in libraries in chapter 1, I review issues associated with developing and planning instruction in chapters 2 through 7. In chapters 8 through 9, I cover characteristics of effective instructors and effective instruction. Chapter 10 is an examination of various methods of assessment. The final chapter distills some of the specific challenges and obstacles faced by librarians providing instruction.

Few would disagree that librarianship is undergoing an identity crisis of sorts. Many traditional models of librarianship and ways of thinking about libraries, librarians, and information are changing radically, are no longer valid, or have simply become obsolete. One thing that has not changed during this period of transition is the need for librarians to provide instruction in the use of information and information resources. In an age when the relevance of libraries is often questioned, bringing effective, meaningful instructional opportunities to library users is more critical than ever. The degree and extent to which librarians are successful in doing so will continue to be crucial in redefining the profession as well as the role of libraries in the educational process and in society at large.

ONE HISTORICAL OVERVIEW OF LIBRARY INSTRUCTION

MANY TERMS HAVE BEEN used over the years to denote and conceptualize instruction involving the library—*bibliographic instruction, library orientation, user education,* and *information instruction,* to name just a few. Strictly speaking, these terms are not interchangeable. They are evolutionary stages as much as models of instruction. Which term is used and how are ultimately often determined as much by the recipients of the instruction as by the library or librarians responsible for providing the instruction. Like other forms of instruction, at the most fundamental of levels all library instruction revolves around two things: content and delivery of that content. Instruction provided by librarians is often a mix incorporating many different topical areas and emphases, particularly given the increasing dependence of both information and libraries upon the use of computer technology. This mix is discussed in greater detail in chapter 5.

Because of this variety, the methods by which instruction is delivered are equally diverse. In fact, if *library instruction* is defined simply as increasing a user's knowledge of a library service or resource, the ways instruction can be delivered are virtually limitless. In this context, for example, a simple brochure outlining call numbers, a conversation with a librarian about interlibrary loan, and a credit-bearing class teaching students how to use information more effectively could all be considered examples of library instruction.

Historically, however one defines and understands it, library instruction has been around as long as there have been libraries. In the United States, at the first American Library Association conference in 1876, Melvil Dewey was among the first to link libraries with schools, implying that librarians held a key part in the education process and were essentially teachers. The role of librarians, the nature of instruction provided by librarians, and the perceptions of librarians as teachers have, however, all changed significantly since Dewey, particularly over the past quarter of a century or so.

To better understand library instruction today, it is useful to have a familiarity with the historical context in which it has emerged and continues to evolve. This is especially true for higher education, where librarians are increasingly being asked to assume a variety of instructional responsibilities and roles. The rest of this chapter provides a broad overview of six key formats for library instruction: bibliographic instruction, library orientation, library instruction, course-integrated instruction, credit-bearing courses, and information literacy instruction.

BIBLIOGRAPHIC INSTRUCTION

Emphasis: Ideas and concepts typically associated with books such as the card catalog, the history of books, and the use/creation of bibliographies.

In 1879, the librarian at the University of Michigan, Raymond C. Davis, was among the first to provide what we today recognize as formalized library instruction. At that time, academic libraries in this country were still essentially storehouses of books and other textual information. They had relatively small collections that typically focused on the liberal arts, especially the humanities. Because of the emphasis on books and the printed word, the early, formalized attempts at instruction typically revolved around bibliographic instruction and focused on things such as the history of books and the use and creation of bibliographies. Davis, for example, observed that students had a limited understanding of libraries and thus instructed them in the use of the card catalog. He also suggested a bibliography course to discuss the history of books and printing and how information was organized in a library.

LIBRARY ORIENTATION

Emphasis: The physical location of items and services. Tours and scavenger hunts are common examples.

Near the end of the 1800s, some significant changes in library operations began to emerge. Up until that time, academic libraries were geared almost exclusively toward faculty. Academic library collections, or *stacks*, were generally not open to students. Students had to ask a librarian for books or other items they wanted. This was often true of public, school, and other libraries as well.

As opening of the stacks to students became more common, instruction began to evolve accordingly. No longer were libraries geared solely to doctoral students or faculty members who learned how to use the library via their course work or personal research. There was now a growing need to educate undergraduate students and others in the use of the library as well. As a result, instruction in the form of library orientation began to appear, with a growing instructional emphasis on the physical arrangement, location, and availability of library items and services.

LIBRARY INSTRUCTION

Emphasis: Addressing "How do I ___?" sorts of questions (e.g., How do I find articles?). This form of instruction often takes the form of a single, general workshop or one-shot instruction session and is geared toward providing awareness of library resources and services and demonstrating how to use them more effectively.

Prior to World War II, libraries struggled to establish instruction programs. Money was often more of a concern than pedagogy, particularly in the late 1920s through the time of the Great Depression. Moreover, at that time only a small percentage of the population attended college. After World War II, though, dramatic changes began to occur in higher education and other areas of society. Enrollments increased significantly, and the "space race" of the 1950s brought additional attention to the desirability of higher education. These and other developments resulted in legislation and budgets that were more supportive of colleges and universities.

As a direct result, many libraries experienced a growth spurt. This growth necessitated that the entire library be incorporated into instruction. Tours and orientations alone were simply no longer adequate to meet the growing needs and changing demands of library users. Unfortunately, demand often exceeded supply. Many libraries did not have the staff or resources to provide all of the instruction needed or even requested. And yet, by the 1960s, at least the idea of librarians providing instruction was increasingly common. It was at that time that such instruction began to be referred to as *library instruction* and to emphasize a more composite, holistic perspective on the library. This model of instruction is still evident in many libraries today in the form of workshops or "one-shots" wherein a class or group of people is given a single, broad exposure to critical library resources, tools, and services.

COURSE-INTEGRATED INSTRUCTION

Emphasis: Instruction in the use of library resources and services needed to address specific assignment- or course-based needs over time.

Unlike library instruction, which typically takes place in a single session, course-integrated instruction takes place over an extended period, usually for the duration of an entire class, allowing for more in-depth exploration of topics and concepts, particularly those related specifically to the course. Library instruction suffers from the fact that it is necessarily broad in scope and often occurs only once. Its one-size-fits-all approach means that specific needs of some individuals are not addressed and that different topics are given different amount of time and emphasis. Moreover, time spent lecturing necessarily reduces time available for experiential and other forms of learning. The lack of subsequent follow-up sessions only exacerbates these problems.

The notion that instruction should take place over time is central to the work of Patricia Bryan Knapp. Seen as one of the foremothers of modern library instruction, Knapp was initially concerned about the quality of undergraduate papers. To address this problem, she was among the first to call for a departure from the one-shot library orientation model. Instead, she advocated the development of competence over a period of time and focused on broader concepts such as the organization of information, the identification of core works, and the importance of evaluating and interpreting information.

Developed in the 1960s, the Earlham College model, as it is sometimes known, builds upon these notions. Similar to library instruction as described above, the focus is on integrating instruction into existing courses. But this model places greater emphasis on faculty-librarian collaborations, instruction taking place throughout the duration of the course, and meeting the specific needs of the students in the course. The model comprises three primary components: *integration*, which sees instruction embedded in courses requiring the use of the library's resources and services; *demonstration*, the primary mode of instruction; and *gradation*, where instruction is a process that take places over time.

CREDIT-BEARING COURSES

Summary: College or other credit is awarded for taking a specialized course focused on a broad cross section of topics related to libraries and information. The topics discussed and focus of the course vary and are dependent on various departmental or institutional needs and expectations.

The focus on student needs and emphasis on the idea that instruction should take place over an extended period formed the foundation of the so-called grassroots movement of the 1960s. Perhaps more significant, it also moved instruction from a task-oriented approach to one that was more process driven; credit-bearing courses emerged that were more reflective of actual research, itself a process that takes place over time and involves many tools, resources, and strategies. Such courses also enabled instructors to go into greater depth about different topics and ideas as well as demonstrate how they are related.

One of the first to call for separate, librarian-taught courses was Daniel Gore. In 1964 he outlined a basic one-semester course that he felt could be taught by any librarian. His proposal incorporated elements of all of the aforementioned methods and approaches in terms of both pedagogy and content.

INFORMATION LITERACY INSTRUCTION

Summary: Rather than being embedded into a specific course or department, this process-based, collaborative form of instruction is incorporated into the entire curriculum, is often provided by more than one department, and may or may not directly involve librarians.

During the 1980s and 1990s, computer technology was making growing amounts of information available in a variety of formats. In essence, information was no longer the sole territory of libraries and librarians. In this broader context in which information was no longer a library-specific commodity, calls for information literacy instruction began to emerge, and increasing references to such began to appear in the literature.

Reflecting this trend, the notion that information literacy instruction needed to be embedded throughout the curriculum (not just within the library or as a set of specific classes or disciplines) grew more common. In 1994, for example, San Jose State University was among the first to develop a campuswide information literacy program—the Information Literacy Initiative—to meet student needs for new skills for the twenty-first century. Standards such as the Association of College and Research Libraries' (ACRL) Information Literacy Competency Standards for Higher Education (2000) and Objectives for Information Literacy Instruction (2001) provided academic librarians and faculty members with the tools to work collaboratively to incorporate information literacy into the curriculum.

Arguably the defining moment in information literacy instruction was the creation and adoption of the Information Literacy Competency Standards for Higher Education. Approved by the ACRL board of directors in January 2000, these five standards establish a framework for instruction as well as a series of outcomes and performance indicators to facilitate inclusion in virtually any curriculum. The five standards describe an information-literate individual as one who (1) determines the nature and extent of the information needed; (2) accesses needed information effectively and efficiently; (3) evaluates information and its sources critically and incorporates selected information into his or her knowledge base and value system; (4) individually or as a member of a group, uses information effectively to accomplish a specific purpose; and (5) understands many of the economic, legal, and social issues surrounding the use of information and accesses and uses information ethically and legally.

LOOKING AHEAD

The evolution of instruction involving librarians has paralleled changes in libraries and librarianship, in what people expect and need from libraries, and in the ways we access and use information. Its multidisciplinary, collaborative, process-oriented approach to information and instruction holds great promise, but even information literacy instruction may ultimately be only another passing stage. As new resources, new services, and new ways of accessing information emerge, instruction will need to evolve accordingly if it is to meet the emergent needs of library users.

TWO WHO TEACHES?

IN THE LITERATURE AND in the workplace, more and more attention is being given to instruction and the teaching role of librarians. Librarians are increasingly responsible for teaching, shaping instruction, and the curricular process. This trend is particularly evident where information literacy programs and activities are being implemented throughout a curriculum or institution. Many reference transactions have added an instructional element. Perhaps the best evidence of all can be seen in the growing emphasis on teaching in job postings and position announcements.

Some characterize this shift in emphasis as an attempt to add legitimacy and credibility to the profession. Many library users have difficulty differentiating between librarians and other library staff members, to a large extent because the respective roles and responsibilities of each are often unclear. Further exacerbating the problem are emerging trends such as the outsourcing of technical services and the decline in the number of questions being asked at the reference desk. By incorporating instruction and performing duties that are familiar and of value to those outside the confines of the library, some librarians hope to make their value more transparent.

Another possible explanation is simply that there is a growing need for instruction. The amount of information continues to expand as the means of access to and formats of information proliferate. The skills needed to succeed academically in today's "knowledge economy" must follow suit. In short, individuals need to know how to access and utilize information more effectively and more efficiently. Librarians are often at the forefront of providing such instruction to meet this ongoing need.

And yet, despite this growing emphasis on instruction, it is important to observe that a large number of librarians who provide instruction still do not have official teaching credentials—that is, they lack formal degrees or backgrounds in education.

In fact, many have little or even no formal classroom teaching experience prior to becoming librarians. Despite these facts, courses about library instruction are limited in most graduate programs, if such courses are even present at all.

As a result, what most librarians know about instruction is based on simple trial-and-error and firsthand experience with what is effective and what is not. Others gain knowledge through conferences, workshops, and other professional development opportunities. In both instances, it may be years, if ever, before this rather piecemeal approach enables an individual to become effective at developing and administering instruction.

RESPONSIBILITY FOR INSTRUCTION

How, then, does an individual become an instruction librarian? Most libraries have some sort of protocol or structure in place delineating exactly how instructional duties are to be assigned. Responsibility for instruction is typically either centralized in one person or a small group of individuals, or decentralized among several individuals. However, even among those for whom instruction is their only or primary responsibility, it is not uncommon to find them working with another librarian or faculty member to provide instruction. Librarians also volunteer to teach on a temporary basis.

Centralized

Centralized instruction is that in which one person or a small group of individuals is specifically assigned to provide instruction. Instruction is a formally designated responsibility and is the primary—possibly the only—responsibility of these librarians. For them, the emphasis on instruction is often reflected in terms such as *instruction* or *education* being part of their job titles or otherwise figuring prominently in their position descriptions. These individuals are typically assigned to handle all aspects of instruction, from developing assignments to providing instruction to conducting assessments and more.

There is no guarantee that greater exposure to teaching or more time in the classroom leads to a higher quality of instruction. But, as a rule, because these librarians are focused primarily on instruction, they necessarily have more experience with teaching and tend to have a broader awareness of curricular issues and trends. In turn, this can translate into greater confidence, passion for teaching, and comfort providing instruction. Centralizing instruction in one person or a select group of individuals facilitates various administrative elements of instruction as well. For example, it is clear to whom requests for instruction, questions, and so on are to be directed.

Unfortunately, because of declining budgets and other factors, not every library can afford to have someone restricted solely to providing instruction. In addition, there may not be enough requests for instruction to warrant a specialized, dedicated person to provide instruction. On the other hand, the workload may be too much for a single person to handle effectively or efficiently. For these reasons, many libraries have adopted a *distributed* model wherein instruction is but one of many assigned responsibilities.

Distributed

In the distributed model, instruction is still an assigned responsibility. But rather than being a librarian's only responsibility, it is simply one of several duties (e.g., collection development, reference) for which the librarian is responsible. Instruction may or may not be the librarian's primary responsibility. This model is often seen in smaller libraries where it is impractical to dedicate someone to instruction only.

One of the biggest benefits of the distributed model is that it can generate another layer of credibility to library instruction. The more individuals involved with instruction, the more likely people perceive instruction as important. Also, having more instructors makes it easier to generate greater awareness of the library's instruction program. Yet this can easily backfire. When librarians are not permitted to teach or all librarians do not have responsibilities for providing instruction, both the perceived and the actual value and roles of librarians in the educational process—both inside the library and out—can be significantly compromised.

Not being assigned instruction duties can be a double-edged sword on a personal level as well. Teaching can be a significant source of stress and anxiety for someone who does not want to teach or is not comfortable doing so. Not being assigned to teach, these people can breathe easier. But for those who want to teach, not being given an opportunity to do so can be a significant source of frustration and professional dissatisfaction.

It is not, however, always possible to assign responsibility for instruction to everyone who would like to teach. Budgetary limitations and the need for instruction are certainly key considerations. The people assigning responsibilities (e.g., dean, library director, department head) may also have to deal with factors outside of their control. Contracts and collective bargaining agreements, for example, may clearly delineate positions, duties, and so on. As a result, some librarians may be prohibited from teaching, particularly if not defined as "faculty" or "instructors." Contract language or limitations may preclude librarians from teaching anything beyond basic library workshops and orientations (i.e., non-credit-bearing courses), if they are permitted to teach at all.

DELEGATION OF INSTRUCTION

Once a decision has been made about how instructional duties are to be assigned, a decision is then made about how instruction is to be distributed; except in cases where one individual handles all instructional duties, there needs to be a means for deciding specifically which librarian is to provide the actual instruction when more than one individual has responsibility for instruction. Suppose a library has three individuals assigned to provide instruction. If an English professor requests instruction for his class on a Wednesday, there must be a means for deciding which of the three librarians is going to provide the instruction.

Delegating Instruction via Liaisons

Many libraries assign librarians to work with certain departments as liaisons. As a liaison, the librarian assigned to a specific department is typically responsible for coordinating all library activities involving that department or members of that department. Acquiring appropriate resources and materials, promoting library resources and services, and providing instruction are all common liaison activities. For example, a librarian assigned to be the library's liaison to the nursing department might order books, process periodical subscriptions, alert nursing faculty to new services, and teach introductory nursing students how to find articles on nursing.

As liaisons, librarians have a great opportunity to build rapport with a department and its faculty. Attending meetings, processing orders, and similar activities all require interaction with faculty members on a variety of levels. Such activities enable a helpful, growing, two-way familiarity between the librarian and the faculty and department.

In terms of instruction, this approach has several advantages. By typically being more familiar than other librarians with a collection for a given department or discipline, a liaison librarian is usually in a better position to suggest books, journals, and other resources to students as they search for information. The liaison may also be most experienced with the important field-specific resources (e.g., *CINAHL* databases for nursing information). At the same time, by working closely with faculty members from a department, the librarian can develop a familiarity with their assignments and curriculum and gain insight into their expectations. This understanding can be extremely helpful in developing appropriate, meaningful instruction and otherwise helping students with their research.

The often arbitrary nature of this model, though, is problematic. When a librarian has expertise or experience with the discipline to which she is assigned, it is likely that instruction will be improved accordingly. She simply has more knowledge and, in some cases, firsthand experience with the subject that she can incorporate into the lessons. But what if there is more than one librarian with similar backgrounds and expertise within a discipline? How is it decided which of them will be responsible for providing instruction or serving as liaison?

The reverse scenario is a bigger problem. Simply put, there are usually more disciplines than there are librarians with expertise in those disciplines. As a result, a librarian assigned to work with the nursing department, for example, may not have background in, knowledge of, or even an interest in nursing or health. Such a situation can pose any of several significant challenges, especially the first few times a librarian provides instruction. Among other problems, the librarian may simply lack the knowledge to answer specific questions. Lacking content knowledge, the librarian may also have difficulty developing good examples to use in class. This can not only compromise the professionalism and credibility of the librarian but seriously detract from developing an effective instruction session.

Another potential problem this method is subject to is the creation of an uneven distribution of instruction. Some departments naturally have more and varied instruction needs than others. Librarians assigned to those departments necessarily need to commit more time and effort to preparing for and administering instruction. The load can escalate quickly if a librarian is assigned to several high-need departments.

Embedded Librarians

In a variant of the liaison model, a librarian is actually embedded into a course. Rather than being assigned to an entire department, the librarian is assigned to work with a specific course. Although they are not the primary instructors, embedded librarians often attend every class. Other times they simply come in and speak as requested. Either way, the students and the primary instructor recognize the librarian as the go-to librarian for the class.

The focus on a single class enables the librarian to become uniquely aware of the specific challenges and needs of the students and professor. In addition to helping them with other responsibilities such as collection development, being embedded is a great way to increase a librarian's approachability. When a student has a need or question, a librarian is readily available—often in the actual classroom—to respond. Even if they cannot initially visually identify the librarian assigned to their class, students coming to the library have an advantage in that they know who to ask for. At the very least, it is reassuring to know that the librarian is probably more familiar with their class and, therefore, perhaps better able to help them than the other librarians. In turn, students with problems may be more likely to ask questions and seek assistance than students from classes without an assigned librarian.

Embedded librarians can be found in a variety of contexts and classes. Because students in these courses tend to need more individualized attention and greater levels of assistance with information and the research process, being embedded in introductory "Freshman Year Experience" and "College Success" sorts of classes is common. But embedded librarians are also placed in upper-level classes. They are typically assigned to classes where they can best employ the combination of their unique background and experiences with a particular subject or issue outside of librarianship. A librarian with a background in chemistry, for example, may be embedded in a course like "Introduction to Chemistry" or "Literature of Chemistry."

Embedded librarians must, however, be careful not to become marginalized. Because they are typically not the primary instructor, two major problems may arise. When they are not physically present in the classroom, embedded librarians may need to be creative and willing to put forth extra effort to make themselves and the library accessible to students. Providing students with contact information and hours of availability should be the minimum. Other possibilities are course-specific web pages, handouts, finding aids, and tutorials.

A more pervasive problem is being relegated to a support role. By definition, embedded librarians are not the primary instructors for classes. Although they may provide instruction from time to time, they are typically present to answer questions and address issues about the library and the research process as they emerge and otherwise to assist the primary instructor. But an embedded librarian may spend a lot of time just sitting in the classroom, because they do not teach every class or because there may not be many questions. In turn, students may conclude that the value of the librarian is dubious; that he is there simply to babysit. This perception is further reinforced if the librarian is not present and lacks regular, ongoing interaction with the students.

Rotating Instruction by Librarian

Another common way to distribute instruction is through a rotation cycle. Here, a list of librarians charged with providing instruction is created. When the first instruction request is received, it is handled by the first librarian on the list, the second request by the second librarian, and so on. Once all of the librarians on the list have taught, the cycle repeats itself.

This method is extremely easy to understand and to administer. It only requires someone to create, maintain, and monitor the list. It also distributes instruction responsibilities evenly. True, when an entire cycle is not completed, some individuals may end up teaching an additional class. Otherwise, though, everyone on the list teaches the same number of times in a given time period.

Despite its ease of implementation, though, this method does have drawbacks. Perhaps the biggest is that it is difficult to know in advance when and what classes a librarian will be teaching. This obviously makes it difficult to prepare lecture notes, handouts, and other course materials. It often results in scheduling conflicts as well. For example, a librarian might already have a meeting or other activity planned when it is his turn to teach. Further, if he is unable to teach because of other duties, he may be seen as unwilling to accept responsibility, not taking instruction seriously, or not being willing do his fair share, especially if he repeatedly chooses the other activity over instruction.

Scheduling courses this way can also be a problem in cases where multiple class sessions are requested. Say a professor requests a session on a Tuesday and another on the following Thursday. The librarian teaching the Tuesday class may or may not come up in the rotation again to teach the following Thursday. Although most are willing to switch as needed, some librarians may end up teaching more than their fair share. On the other hand, if the librarian does not teach the second and subsequent sessions, there are problems with continuity, oversight, and redundancies: librarian B does not know specifically what librarian A did or did not address in the first session.

Last, although this method can complement a liaison's work with a department, it can just as easily compromise it. As noted above, liaisons are a great way to build rapport with faculty and can be win-win situations for everyone when done well. But this rapport can be damaged when the instruction librarian and the librarian serving as liaison to the department requesting the instruction are not the same librarian. Faculty members, for example, may become confused about who they should go to with a particular question or concern about the library. They may feel more comfortable working and dealing with the instruction librarian than they do with their liaison librarian, or vice versa. These sorts of things can place the liaison librarian, the instruction librarian, or both in an awkward situation and be seen as intruding on one's territory.

Rotating Instruction by Time

Rather than rotate instruction by class, this method rotates instruction by time. First, a schedule of all available time slots for instruction is created. Librarians can then either be assigned to slots or choose the times and days they are willing to teach until all of the slots have been filled. For example, for Mondays, librarian A might choose 9 a.m., librarian B 10 a.m., and so on. When a request for instruction at 10 a.m. on a Monday comes in, the librarian assigned to that time slot is responsible for providing instruction—in this case, librarian B.

In deciding to distribute instruction using this model, one of the key questions to be addressed at the onset is how the available slots are to be filled. At the very least, this means deciding whether librarians choose or are simply placed into slots. In either case, there needs to be a method to decide the selection order. Using seniority or the results of a lottery are common. Similar to the rotation of librarians outlined above, some choose to create a list of librarians and then place the first librarian in the first time slot, the second in the second, and so on. Then, once the list is exhausted, the cycle is repeated until all available slots have been filled.

A related question revolves around the logistics of selection. For example, can a librarian sign up for every available 9 to 10 a.m. slot, or only certain days (e.g., all Wednesdays), or a certain number of days per week, or some combination thereof? Depending on how slots are to be filled, determining for how many slots each librarian is responsible also needs to be determined. Likewise, it needs to be made clear whether or not a librarian can sign up for all of his slots at one time or if turns are to be taken with the other librarians.

When librarians are able to choose, a couple of key benefits can result. For one, it gives librarians a sense of empowerment to be able to choose when to teach. The problem of double-booking is also virtually eliminated, since librarians can schedule instruction around meetings and other activities. For example, if a librarian knows she may be expected to teach at 9 a.m. on Tuesdays, she can schedule other activities accordingly. Conversely, if she knows she has a meeting every Wednesday at three o'clock, she should not sign up for instruction at that time.

As is true with other methods, this one also has disadvantages. If they are able to choose their own times, some librarians may purposely choose all of the off-peak slots, anticipating that they will not have to teach much, if at all. When slots are randomly assigned, some may be forced to teach more because they have been assigned peak time slots.

In addition to some of the problems associated with the other methods noted above, this model bypasses any liaison system that might be in place. The librarian teaching the class may not be the liaison assigned to the department and, as a result, may have little to no knowledge of the class, the department, or the subject matter. Consequently, librarians must often spend considerably more time and effort to prepare and teach courses assigned in this way. The relatively arbitrary nature of this model also means that those with expertise in a discipline may not be the ones teaching the classes to which they are best suited.

Coteaching

Coteaching involves two instructors sharing responsibility for providing instruction and combines many of the elements of the models outlined above. The roles and degree of involvement for each instructor vary depending on factors such as number of classes, content, and structure of the course. For example, for a multisession class, the instructors may divide the sessions evenly so that each teaches an equal number. For larger classes, one librarian may serve as the instructor and the other in more of a support capacity.

Regardless of how it is structured, one of the biggest benefits of coteaching is a sharing of the burden. Instead of placing all of the responsibility on one person, the burdens of teaching are shared with at least one other person. Care must be taken, though, to ensure that the burden is shared evenly, or at least that individual responsibilities are clearly articulated. Coordinating this can be particularly challenging. Coordinating two schedules instead of one, for example, can be especially challenging, particularly if instruction is to be provided for more than one session. For these and other reasons, frequent, ongoing communication is imperative if cotaught courses are to be effective, even more so when both instructors are not librarians.

Coteaching with Another Librarian

The reasons for coteaching with another librarian are many and varied. It might simply be that the class is very large and having a second librarian present helps maintain discipline and expedite the class. One librarian may be in front of the class teaching while the other helps ensure that disruptions to the actual lesson are minimized. In this capacity, the second instructor serves in more of a support role by doing things like helping to keep students on task and addressing individual equipment problems that might arise. Depending on need and the nature of the class, sometimes roles are reversed: the librarian serving as primary instructor for class A may be the secondary instructor for class B. Such reversals may be temporary or may be in place for the duration of the class.

Scenarios where the primary instructor lacks experience with or expertise on a given topic or resource or where it is desirable to have a second perspective are also suitable for coteaching. In both situations, the second instructor serves much as a guest speaker, addressing specific issues and concepts as designated by the primary instructor. This is often seen where specialized topics or technologies are being discussed. One might call in the cataloging librarian when discussing call numbers and the arrangement of items in the collection. Or the librarian in charge of nonprint media might come in to speak about the library's multimedia resources and services.

In libraries where librarians have multiple duties, coteaching with a fellow librarian can be problematic. This is particularly true when one librarian lacks teaching experience or a desire to teach. Among other things, a second librarian involved with a class necessarily has less time to work on other projects or duties. This can create both personal and professional rifts and may otherwise disrupt various aspects of the day-to-day operation of the library. When attempting to determine if coteaching is desirable, one must weigh the advantages to be gained against what will be lost. In the end, it may be just as effective to have the second librarian serve as more of a consultant, providing instruction in very specific instances, rather than as a regular teacher assigned to the class on an ongoing basis.

Coteaching with a Faculty Member

Instead of a librarian, sometimes the second instructor is a faculty member. In this case, the librarian is typically not the primary instructor, but this method differs from the embedded librarian scenario in that the primary role is instruction rather than working with every aspect of a given class. Coteaching with a faculty member is common in upper-level courses requiring research or the use of obscure or complex resources. Here, the team works in tandem, with the faculty member focusing on delivering content while the librarian instructs students on accessing and using course-relevant library resources and services.

Although it is different from embedding, coteaching with a faculty member often suffers the same shortcomings. Among others, the workload may not be distributed evenly, and the librarian may serve primarily in a support capacity or may not be involved with curricular matters (e.g., developing assignments). Librarians finding themselves in this situation need to examine their roles and contributions to the class candidly to see if an alternative approach (e.g., teaching when requested) might be more appropriate.

Volunteering

For some, teaching is done on a voluntary basis; it is not part of their regular duties or a formal responsibility of their position. This can be a one-shot opportunity or a longer-term commitment such as teaching a credit-bearing course. It can also be self-initiated or in response to a request for instruction. A library may maintain a list of those willing to teach, or individuals may be asked to volunteer as the need arises.

Allowing those to teach who want to has several benefits. It can be empowering and gratifying to be allowed to do what you want to do. For libraries that do not have large staffs, it can be a way to expand or enhance existing instruction opportunities. For administrators, it can be a way to save money, and it enables librarians normally assigned to teach to do other things.

Allowing volunteers to teach, though, may create more problems than it solves. First and foremost, not everyone who wants to teach is qualified to do so. This has two sides. If the volunteer is more effective than the librarian assigned to teach, any of a number of personal or professional problems are likely to emerge. On the other hand, if the volunteer is ineffective, the natural question is why she was allowed to provide instruction in the first place. In addition, there may not be enough need for those assigned to teach, much less for those who volunteer to do so. Even if there is, there may be contractual or personal issues with volunteers doing work paid staff are supposed to be doing.

THREE HOW STUDENTS LEARN

WHEN YOU ARE DEVELOPING and administering instruction, it is important to keep in mind that everyone learns differently. Some students learn best by "doing"; for others, lecture alone is sufficient. For this reason, librarians providing instruction should try to incorporate a variety of presentation techniques and learning activities into their lessons. In demonstrating how to search a database for articles, for example, a librarian should consider embedding some sort of hands-on, experiential component as a supplement to a straight lecture about how to conduct the search.

Unfortunately, time is typically the biggest hurdle to overcome in attempting to address this issue. This is particularly true for classes that meet with a librarian only once. No matter how it is presented, there is often barely enough time to cover all of the desired content. To accommodate multiple modes of learning as well is difficult at best. Exacerbating the problem is the fact that many instruction librarians have other responsibilities beyond instruction. As a result, they simply do not have time to develop and incorporate a variety of teaching styles and learning activities into their lessons.

To be truly effective, instructors need to not only examine their own practices but also learn more about the factors that affect how students learn. Some key things to consider about student learning and the learning process are learning theories, learning styles, and the common obstacles to learning.

LEARNING THEORIES

Learning theories attempt to describe how people learn. Librarians certainly do not need to be psychologists to understand learning theories. It is, however, important for librarians to be aware that how one learns is a complex process that no single theory can explain. In fact, some would argue that there is no need for learning theories, that they create more problems than they solve in that they make too many assumptions about too many things to be practical.

Others, though, argue that learning theories are valuable. They suggest that instructors at least examine how they are teaching and consider incorporating various elements of different learning theories when developing lectures, handouts, presentation styles, and other elements of instruction. There are many different theories about how individuals learn; three of the more commonly recognized models are behaviorism, cognitivism, and constructivism.

Behaviorism. For a true behaviorist, there is no such thing as consciousness or internal mental states. Behaviorists focus on observable behavior. Learning takes place only when a behavior change is observable. One key concept of behaviorism is the notion of classical conditioning, in which a response is paired with a stimulus. Another theory revolves around operant conditioning, in which reinforcement is used to encourage or discourage behavior. Key behaviorists include Tolman Bandura, Clark L. Hull, C. Lloyd Morgan, Ivan Pavlov, B. F. Skinner, Edward Thorndike, and John B. Watson.

Cognitivism. Theories of cognitivism assume that mental processes (e.g., memory), beliefs, and personal experiences influence learning. Cognitivists believe that learners are not just responding to their environment but are rational beings who must actively participate in order to learn. Meaning is constructed by individuals, and learning can take place without any form of reinforcement. Key cognitivists include J. R. Anderson, Robert M. Gagne, Jean Piaget, R. C. Shank, and Edward Tolman.

Constructivism. The basic precept of constructivism is that individuals create ("construct") their own meaning through reflection on prior knowledge and personal experiences. The result is a *mental model* that is both contextualized and subjective. Learning is an active, often self-initiated process that results from adjustments to mental models as we encounter new experiences. Key constructivists include J. Bruner, John Dewey, Maria Montessori, Piaget, and L. S. Vygotsky.

LEARNING STYLES

Whereas a learning theory attempts to describe how individuals learn, a learning style applies specifically to an individual. The term emerged in the 1970s and simply refers to an individual's approach to or way of learning. Each of us processes information and learns in a variety of ways, but most individuals have a primary mode through which they learn best; this primary mode is referred to as one's learning style.

There are a variety of definitions and models of learning styles, but all are based on how we experience and interpret the world. Many models see learning styles on a sort of continuum. Abstract versus concrete thinking is an example. This dichotomy recognizes that some are better able to understand concepts (abstract), and others learn better by doing or applying what they have been taught (concrete). Some other dichotomies are logic/emotion, reflection/practice, divergent/convergent, and sensing/thinking.

A related concept is that of *multiple intelligences*. Here, learners are grouped into broad categories based on how they learn best. The theory suggests that intelligence is not a single, unified concept but rather a series of interconnected ones. It is believed that visual learners, for example, tend to think in pictures or imagery and learn best through instruction methods that include visual elements such as handouts. Spatial learners, on the other hand, learn best by perceiving or creating images. Other categories of intelligence include verbal, musical, bodily, interpersonal, intrapersonal, and naturalistic.

ROADBLOCKS TO LEARNING

Just as students learn in different ways and a variety of factors influence the learning process, there are a variety of elements that can inhibit learning. Some of these can be addressed by the instructor, but many cannot. Just as no instructor could possibly accommodate all students' learning styles, it is also impossible to cover all of the possible contingencies, problems, or challenges students are likely to encounter. Moreover, some of these issues do not emerge until a class is under way and are, therefore, impossible to anticipate.

In any given class, the instructor needs to use judgment in deciding whether to deal with these issues and, if so, which ones and to what depth. In some cases, discussing problems may create more confusion than it resolves. As a general rule, instructors should try to establish a middle ground and talk about global problems or problems that occur with some regularity, and then address the "extremes" only as time and circumstances permit.

Technology-Related Concerns

As the dependence on information technology continues to increase, the number of emergent technology-based problems continues to rise as well. Unfortunately, when a problem is reported or experienced, its origin is not always clear. It could be a user error, a problem with the student's local machine, a default setting or configuration issue, a problem with the host site of the resource or service, or some combination thereof. The volume and variety of possible scenarios make it difficult to develop lesson plans and instructional materials.

For that reason alone, instructors need to decide how much, if any, attention to devote to these problems. Although the answer to some specific problem might seem straightforward, it can quickly blossom into other concerns or problems. For example, library users can still come to the library to do their work, but more and more expect to access library resources remotely. As a result, although it is not necessary to discuss how to log in to resources remotely, it is probably something worth mentioning in class. But this leads to any of a number of related issues, such as the possible need to reset one's password, known browser issues, or licensing restrictions to off-site content or features. This further decreases the amount of time available to spend on more universal content needs and topics.

Previous Experience

Previous experiences strongly influence a student's ability to learn. Clearly bad experiences tend to have a negative impact. But even a positive experience may no longer be appropriate. For example, a student might have had good instruction as a freshman. But now, as a senior, what he learned may no longer be accurate, or he may have needs that were not present or apparent three years earlier. Three experience-related elements are outlined below. Instruction librarians need to be aware of such roadblocks and develop instruction accordingly.

Technology vs. Information Skills

Everyone comes to class with different levels of experience and expertise with respect to both the necessary technologies and the research process. Some students have excellent technological skills but difficulty transferring them to the research process. Others have strong research and information skills but lack the technological skills to conduct research effectively and efficiently. Most students fall somewhere in between.

Libraries and Librarians

Some students have had considerable experience with libraries and librarians, others very little. Regardless, it is not realistic to assume that all of these experiences have been positive. Sometimes it is a matter of personality. It is a simple fact that some librarians are more helpful and more approachable than others. Unfortunately, when students encounter a less approachable librarian, their impression is likely to be generalized to other librarians. Worse, they are likely to share their impressions with other students and be more hesitant about interacting with a librarian in the future.

A growing number of students are unclear about the role of a librarian in the first place. Some cannot distinguish between library staff and librarians. They may approach a staff member with a simple question, and the staff member may have no idea how to help them.

A bigger issue is the ever-expanding availability of remote resources and services. In short, a growing number of library users feel little need to come to the library. In turn, because students can do their own work, the number of interactions with librarians continues to change and, in many cases, decline. When students do interact, it is just as likely to be about a technology-related issue as it is a traditional library-related one.

Transferable Instruction

There can be problems of transferability: what is learned about one library may or may not be appropriate to another library. For example, what a student learns about using a particular school library may not be applicable to a public or academic library. Different resources, different classification schemes (e.g., Dewey vs. Library of Congress), and so on can make transitioning problematic.

Technologies and resources change all of the time. As a result, what was learned even yesterday may no longer be valid. Some of these changes are initiated by libraries. Changing the name or location of a resource link is not uncommon. In other cases the changes are beyond the library's control. Vendors, for example, may change a particular resource's interface or add new features and functionality. Instruction librarians must constantly look for and monitor such changes to help ensure that their lessons are as current as possible.

Not all students receive instruction, and not all students receive the same instruction. Some are taught a few things but in great detail; others are taught a lot of things in a cursory manner. Some instructors provide students with the specific skills they need to complete a particular class or assignment but do not explain how such skills might apply to other contexts. Other students are taught broad, conceptual sorts of things but have no idea how to apply them in real-life situations.

For instruction librarians, the key challenge here is finding a balance. Elementary presentations risk being redundant and so basic that they bore everyone. Yet an advanced presentation is equally ineffective if the concepts and techniques discussed are so sophisticated or complex as to lack context or make it difficult for students to replicate. Instructors need to acknowledge that they are going to "lose" some students at both ends of the spectrum and focus on developing instruction that meets the needs and expectations of the majority who fall in the middle.

FOUR PREDELIVERY CONSIDERATIONS

A KEY COMPONENT OF any class is development of content. But instruction involves more than just developing and presenting content to an audience. Before one actually begins delivering a class, decisions should be made or at least weighed on numerous other aspects of the education process—delivery platform, level of formality, class size, reliance on equipment, and methods of registration, among others. Unfortunately, many librarians are often unaware of these considerations or neglect to deal with them in the planning and development phase.

DELIVERY PLATFORM

The platform for delivery needs to be considered early on in the development phase. Three options—direct, indirect, and hybrids—are summarized below. Instructors need to make conscious decisions about which platform is best suited to them and their respective audience. The interpersonal aspects of direct delivery, for example, present numerous advantages. But delivering such courses is rather inflexible in that it requires students to be physically present at the time and location of the class. Conversely, indirect delivery generally provides greater flexibility. However, such courses may present a significant learning curve to the individuals developing and administering them.

Direct Delivery

This is the traditional style of instruction where the students and the instructor occupy the same space at the same time. Equating this method with face-to-face instruction is not entirely accurate. Technologies such as ITV allow a professor to be "present" but in a virtual sense. Either way, though, the defining element of direct delivery is that the instructor has some sort of tangible presence in the class. Although it is changing, this style is still the most familiar to most people, particularly older students. It is also typically most familiar to instructors, making it easier for them to generate content and otherwise envision the big picture.

In these classes, questions and answers are presented in real time. This results in responses to questions and problems being direct and immediate. That and the fact that students and instructors can interact during every class enable direct-delivered courses to be great rapport-building experiences for students, instructors, and librarians alike.

Direct-delivered courses do, however, have drawbacks. Perhaps the most obvious is that students need to be present at the time and place of the class to receive instruction. When students are absent, they miss critical learning opportunities. Moreover, instruction delivered in this way is virtually impossible to replicate. Even instructors teaching multiple sections of the same class rarely say exactly the same thing to every class or present material in exactly the same manner.

The structure of direct-delivered courses may also create problems. For example, it may not be as appealing to some because of its dependence on place and time. This is likely to become increasingly true for younger students who have experienced increasing levels of instruction online or through other electronic means. Along the same lines, the pace and sequence of a direct-delivered course are set by the instructor. To some extent, this is true in courses delivered indirectly as well. But the rigid pacing of face-to-face courses can be a significant impediment to the ways students learn and the speed at which they progress through a course.

Indirect Delivery

With courses delivered indirectly, the instructor is not necessarily physically present while students are receiving instruction. Such courses are also not bound by a particular place or time. Common examples of this type of delivery include courses administered via the Internet, an intranet, or a learning management system (e.g., E-College, Blackboard, D2L). Some classes and programs may incorporate some sort of face-to-face requirement, but this is minimal and often takes place early, usually in the form of an orientation (e.g., how to access the course), or at the end (e.g., final examination). Interactions between students and instructors may take place in real time or be delayed.

The structure of courses delivered indirectly has advantages. For students, the ability to take a class any place, any time, is appealing. Depending on how the instructor has produced the course, students can proceed through many, sometimes all elements at their own pace. Compared to courses delivered directly, instruction delivered indirectly tends to be more consistent every time the course is taught. In addition to consistency, there are advantages to the instructor as well. For example, instructors can link students quickly, easily, and directly to course content and activities. At the same time, they can usually manage when content (e.g., tests, notes) appears or is available.

Still, this method of delivery is not without its problems. In some cases the instructor may need to become familiar with new software and hardware to develop, participate in, or administer the class. For first-time instructors, the amount of time needed to develop an online class successfully should not be underestimated. But even for experienced instructors, developing an online course may require considerable time and effort to translate face-to-face content and elements adequately and appropriately into a corresponding online experience. Unfortunately, some elements simply may not translate well, if at all. Even when they do, technical configurations on a student's personal computer may render certain aspects of a course problematic or even impossible to access and utilize effectively for that student.

There are also pedagogical concerns. For one, students may struggle with how to use course software appropriately, which obviously impacts how much and how well they are able to learn. As a result, instructors may need to spend considerable time explaining to students how to access course material, participate in class discussions, and so on.

Even students who are comfortable using the technology face challenges. Because they typically do not have physical access to their instructor, students taking courses delivered indirectly necessarily interact with their instructor in different ways. They may do things like post questions to a bulletin board or place assignments in a virtual drop box. But just because a student is working on an assignment at a particular time does not mean that the instructor is available at that time to answer questions or offer guidance. This can be frustrating to students who are used to or need immediate feedback. Moreover, because the interaction is often through virtual means such as online posts or e-mail messages, it may take several interactions before the instructor understands the question or problem and helps resolve it.

Hybrid Delivery

So-called hybrid delivery incorporates both direct and indirect elements outlined above. Such courses are commonplace and are likely to increase in the future. Because they blend elements of these two delivery methods, they gain the advantages of each. Although they also suffer from the disadvantages, they are often not as problematic as those delivered as strictly direct or indirect courses.

Because they are hybrid, such courses offer instructors numerous opportunities that are not necessarily present in the same way or to the same degree as in their nonhybrid counterparts. How hybrid courses are structured and delivered is entirely up to the instructor. Some instructors place more emphasis on one element than another; others attempt to find a suitable balance. For example, some instructors may present content via a face-to-face lecture but have handouts, class notes, and other supporting material posted online for students to access at their leisure.

LEVEL OF FORMALITY

The level or degree of formality is a qualitative measure of the way a student participates in the instruction. Some students work better at their own pace, discovering their own answers in their own way. Other students need more structure; they need someone else to organize and present the content. Most libraries provide some combination of formal and informal instructional opportunities.

Informal activities are those that students engage in on their own. They are able to look for and find answers independently. Participation in this type of instruction is typically voluntary. Moreover, students are generally able to do this at their own pace. People who are self-motivated or reluctant to ask for help may migrate to these opportunities more than to others. Informal instruction is provided through such things as brochures, online tours, handbooks, tutorials, web pages, information kiosks, workbooks, signage, and resource help screens.

In contrast, formal instructional activities require some form of scheduling. The content and pace of such classes are established by the instructor. Formal instruction may be scheduled by the students themselves or may be part of a larger curriculum (e.g., credit-bearing courses). Students, for example, may sign up for a workshop on how to use the catalog to find books. However, it is equally likely that a primary instructor requests instruction for an entire class. In this instance, students are required to attend the class. The originating professor may assign attendance points or require the completion of an assignment based on the lecture to encourage attendance. A teacher requiring students to do research on poetry might schedule an instruction session to teach how to use library resources to find information on poets and poetry. The six main formats for formal instruction are outlined in chapter 1. Typical examples of formal instruction are single-session classes or workshops, multisession classes or series of workshops, and one-on-one instruction sessions.

CLASS SIZE

Although smaller classes are generally more desirable on several levels, the size of an actual class may not be something over which the librarian has control. When they do have options, teaching librarians must decide the optimal number of students for whatever instruction they intend to provide. Smaller class sizes provide opportunities for more individualized instruction based on specific student needs and expectations, but such instruction is inefficient. It is far more efficient to deal with one class of twenty students than to schedule twenty individualized instruction sessions, particularly for general, universal sorts of concepts and content.

In many instances, though, the librarian has no choice about class size. For example, a professor might want to bring a class of fifty students to the library for instruction. Many librarians are reluctant to reject such requests outright, but large classes can pose problems the instruction librarian must address. Content and pedagogy aside, there may simply not be enough seating in the library classroom to accommodate a large group. The librarian could split his presentation in half and do two abbreviated sessions during the allotted time period. But this necessarily means that some things are not covered or are covered less thoroughly than originally intended. In such a case, the librarian could ask for a second session during which he repeats his presentation to those who do not attend the first class. But because of the disruption to the sequencing and flow of their class, many classroom teachers do not consent to multiple full-length sessions.

SELECTING AND USING APPROPRIATE TECHNOLOGY

It needs to be said that using technology to administer a class does not necessarily mean that the class or instruction will be good or made better. Technology is just a tool. Instructors need to determine what they want to do and decide whether the use of specific tools will enable them to accomplish it more effectively. In this context, incorporating too much technology can be just as bad, if not worse, than not using any technology at all and vice versa. For example, the need for the instructor to be present is negligible if all she is doing is reading PowerPoint slides. Such a presentation could simply be posted somewhere students can view it at their leisure. On the other hand, if the class is large or if the classroom makes it difficult to hear, it would be remiss for an instructor not to consider the use of a microphone to help ensure that everyone can hear.

In the end, decisions about which tools, if any, are to be used in a class, and how they are to be used, should at the very last be based on the instructor's needs, the objectives of the course, and the tools available. Again, the world's best technology can do little to improve the quality of an unorganized or inappropriate lecture. Conversely, the lack of technology does not mean that learning cannot take place or that students will be disengaged. The best classes and the best instructors use relevant technology and use it appropriately.

AWARENESS VS. APPLICATION

Awareness can be equated with "knowing what." The emphasis is on making students aware of a resource or service. *Application,* on the other hand, can be equated with "knowing how." Here, the focus is on learning how to do something, and in this case instruction tends to be more structured, more sequential. In an awareness class, the emphasis might be on learning what the catalog is and where it can be accessed; in an application class, the focus would be on learning how to use the catalog to find books.

Most instruction attempts to include elements of both awareness and application. Unfortunately, the more time one spends talking about what is available, typically the less time there is for demonstrating how to use it. Primarily because of time constraints, many one-shot workshops, for example, must often revolve around developing an awareness of what is available. Often there simply is not enough time to go into any great detail about how to use a particular resource. Finding the appropriate balance is a crucial challenge that must be addressed.

ADVERTISING AND MARKETING

Although advertising classes in the library is certainly a good idea, it should not be the only place you make your offerings known. Particularly in an age of remote access to library resources and services, those likely to want or need classes may not actually be in the library much, if at all. For that reason, classes should be advertised in places most likely to be encountered by the appropriate audience. Some of these venues are student and community newspapers; radio and television; Internet; the library newsletter, calendar, bulletin board, and information kiosk; and e-communication (e.g., e-mail, blogs, wikis, social networks).

At its core, marketing is essentially the process of planning, developing, promoting, and distributing a product or service to satisfy organizational goals. Even though many librarians are comfortable advertising their classes, marketing often gets overlooked or makes people uncomfortable. Obviously, if people are not aware that classes are available, they do not enroll in them. But effective marketing is about more than just putting up a sign or sending an e-mail to an instructor that classes are being offered. It involves creating value, conveying that value to others, and, ultimately, convincing them that instruction is worthwhile.

Librarians should not be expected to be marketing experts, but it can help them to understand a handful of basic concepts and ideas that go into successful marketing efforts. In turn, this understanding can be used to evaluate, plan, market, and administer both classes and an overall program of instruction more effectively. Three critical, related considerations are outlined here.

Know Your Product

Although it may seem obvious, to market what you have to offer you first have to *understand* what exactly it is that you are offering. For instruction librarians, the product or service being provided is essentially instruction. But what exactly does that mean? What is instruction? Saying "The library does instruction" or "Librarians teach classes" may mean or be perceived as something completely different to someone outside the library. The term *instruction* may even be ambiguous to librarians who do not provide instruction on a regular basis.

Answering basic questions such as "Are you providing credit-bearing courses or walk-in workshops?" and "Will your class be more lecture-based or hands-on/experiential?" is critical in developing a common understanding of library instruction. Individuals need this basic sort of understanding before they can decide to enroll in a class. Answering such questions is even more critical in attempting to market your classes, particularly at institutions where the librarians are not faculty members or are not perceived as teachers. To a large extent, the success of an individual class as well as of an overall program of instruction depends upon the degree to which you clearly and succinctly articulate what you are offering.

Know Your Market

Students are the most obvious and direct market, but it is important to note that they are not the only market. Albeit in different ways and to different degrees, there are other individuals such as parents and administrators who should not be overlooked when you are marketing library instruction. These individuals are often critical in funding, scheduling, student selection of courses, and more. Thus, it is a good idea periodically to examine the types of materials and information being requested by and shared with these individuals to help ensure that your library instruction is in line with their expectations and needs.

That said, students and faculty members who request instruction on behalf of an entire class of students are often the primary market for library instruction. Understanding their needs and expectations is especially critical. Not only does doing so allow for an appropriate and effective presentation, it also helps you modify existing classes and develop new ones down the road to meet emergent needs.

As you attempt to understand the needs and expectations of these central groups, it is important to address several key questions. In answering these questions, instruction librarians can develop their classes to remain relevant and not to become some self-perpetuating service where classes are being held just to hold them.

- What is the best time, day, and location to hold a class?
- What are the desired learning outcomes?
- In what ways can what is learned be useful/applied?
- Are there particular types of individuals, classes, or departments that could benefit from instruction more than others?
- What degree of customization to particular needs is desired?
- What is the attending faculty member's role?

Know Your Product's Value

Along with knowing your product, you must also understand and convey your instruction's value to those who are likely to participate. Looked at another way, instruction librarians need to ask why someone would take their class. Instruction librarians cannot presume significance or that the importance of instruction is self-evident. Although librarians may feel strongly or even have evidence that students need instruction, others may think otherwise and may need to be convinced. This may be especially true at institutions where librarians do not have faculty status or are not seen as teachers.

You may also need to demonstrate how and in what ways the instruction you are providing is different from that offered by the primary faculty member. Why would faculty members schedule a session with a librarian if they can do the instruction themselves on their own schedule in their own way? In the information age, instruction librarians need to be sensitive to the fact that they no longer have a monopoly on information. Arguably, they may have a deeper understanding of available library resources and services. But that does not mean that nonlibrarians cannot develop that understanding on their own.

In the end, this is not to say that librarians should not have a significant stake in the types of instruction being offered. Still, if a program of instruction is to succeed, the customers—students and teachers alike—need to understand the value of the proposed instruction. We live in an age of increasing expectations for accountability and growing demands on diminishing amounts of time and resources. As a result, instruction librarians need not so much to convince others that instruction is important as to show them how such instruction fits in with and meets curricular, departmental, or institutional goals and objectives.

INTERNAL SELF-ASSESSMENT

Instruction takes place on a continuum. Some classes are new, some have been taught a while, and most typically fall somewhere in between. Whether developing a new course or teaching an existing one, instruction librarians need to take an honest look at the classes they teach and where they fall on the continuum. In so doing, they can develop a deeper appreciation of existing courses they teach as well as future possibilities.

From the world of business, the concept of *product life cycle* is helpful in this regard. A product's life cycle is generally seen as consisting of four stages: introduction, growth, maturity, and decline. Because the expectations are different at each stage, the emphases are different as well:

STAGE	EMPHASIS
Introduction	Making people aware of product and getting people to try it
Growth	Getting people to perceive value of product versus not having product
Maturity	Leveraging successes and reducing/eliminating product weaknesses
Decline	Introducing new markets and finding new ways of using old products

In looking to the future, librarians need to understand where existing instruction falls within this cycle to better develop ways of addressing problems, planning future classes, attracting new participants, and otherwise attending to issues associated with their classes.

PRE-ASSESSMENT

Prior to class, instruction librarians often conduct a pre-assessment of participants' skills and knowledge of the content being conveyed. Chapter 10 discusses assessment in greater detail. But it is important to note here that such assessments can have several benefits. Not the least of these is that the data collected can be used to plan one's lectures and handouts. Topics that students seem to understand, for example, can be discussed sparingly or removed from the lecture altogether. Conversely, concepts and ideas that they seem to struggle with can be given greater emphasis.

However, the benefits of pre-assessment need to be weighed against the problems it can generate. One of the key challenges is the time involved. In an hourlong class, spending even five minutes conducting an assessment at the start of a class reduces the time available to provide actual instruction, even more so if there are questions or problems. On the other hand, conducting a pre-assessment prior to the start of class requires additional time, effort, and coordination on the part of the librarian. An even greater burden is placed on the attending faculty member if he is expected to conduct the pre-assessment. If the faculty member is even the least bit hesitant about scheduling an instruction session with a librarian, he is going to be even more so about taking up additional class time conducting an assessment. If the students are asked to complete the pre-assessment voluntarily on their own outside of class, the rate of return may be small, and even those who do complete it may not take it seriously.

Pre-assessments need to be done with clear objectives in mind. Whether to aid in course development, simply as a means of generating information about the demographics of a given class, or for some other reason, the purpose of the assessment should be clear to the librarian as well as the students or faculty members being asked to participate. Collecting data just for the sake of collecting it benefits no one and is a waste of time. If a pre-assessment is to be conducted, it should have a specific purpose and equally clear objectives and outcomes.

REGISTRATION

The librarian needs to provide both a way for faculty or others to submit a request for instruction and a means to track requests. Sometimes students self-register. For example, there might be a sign-up sheet posted outside the classroom door announcing a workshop on using citation software. Other times the classroom instructor coordinates a class with the instruction librarian. Either way, instruction librarians need to provide a means of registering for classes and for managing such requests when they are received. Specific details for such activities are outlined in chapter 7. Some broad topics to consider in the pre-delivery phase include the following four:

Make the process straightforward and simple. The registration process should be succinct. The instructions for registration should be more or less self-explanatory and not involve a lot of registrants' time. If there are directions of some kind, they should be minimal and very clear as to what is needed or expected.

Identify key information to include (or exclude). Every class and context is different. As a result, how much information to include on the registration form (or how little) varies. In some cases, librarians include an abstract, goals and objectives, times, dates, and so on. At the very least, though, contact information should always be provided to assist those who might have questions or need additional information.

Request relevant information. There are many essential elements a registration form should include. The day, date, and time of the request are essential. The reason for the request (e.g., to assist students with a specific assignment), the classroom instructor's contact name, and alternate dates and times are also recommended. To expedite the registration process, superfluous or extraneous information should be excluded whenever possible. Information such as students' grade point averages may be interesting but has absolutely no bearing on the registration process. Requests for information that does not pertain directly to the registration process should be kept to a minimum if it is incorporated at all.

Determine how to handle incomplete or late registrations. No matter how straightforward a registration process is, incomplete forms are often submitted, and requests are submitted after a posted deadline. Instruction librarians need to be prepared to handle such requests. As a rule of thumb, suggesting instruction requests be submitted a week in advance is not unreasonable. This allows the librarian time to follow up with the requestor on missing information (e.g., lack of requested day or time) and to otherwise prepare for the class. If a request is submitted after a deadline, the librarian needs to decide whether to schedule the class. If someone just walks into a class without having registered, the librarian must be ready to allow or not allow participation.

FIVE WHAT TO TEACH

SEVERAL BROAD, IDENTIFIABLE THEMES are typically associated with library instruction. Teaching students how to access and use library resources and services effectively certainly remains at the core of library instruction. Increasingly, though, librarians are being asked to discuss related topics such as the evaluation and citation of source material. In part, this is in response to the changing needs of students in today's Information Age. But it is also in response to a growing expectation to incorporate principles of information literacy into instruction.

CONTENT AREAS

What is taught depends on the nature of the class, the desired learning outcomes, and a variety of other factors. Ultimately, though, content can typically be grouped into one of four broad areas of content emphasis. Classes may revolve around one specific content area, or they may incorporate elements from several different categories as outlined below.

Describing Libraries and Library Resources and Services

The focus here is on such topics as the history and philosophy of libraries and the various resources and services libraries provide. It may be about libraries in general or specific to the library at which the instruction takes place. As part of larger classes, this type of content is often used early to provide context for the remainder of the course. It can also be used to establish a historical context for a current situation or concept. It is also often associated with activities such as tours and scavenger hunts.

Examples

- Provide an overview of the historical development of libraries.
- Discuss the history of the Internet and its impact on both existing and future libraries.
- Describe existing library resources and services.

Accessing/Acquiring Information

This category has two levels. First is teaching others how to use library resources and services to find the information that is needed. At the same time, though, it means providing the concepts and skills needed to actually acquire the desired items. It is important to note that the two are not necessarily the same, but because many of the concepts in this area are interdependent, they are often discussed concurrently.

Examples

- Demonstrate how to create a resource list using an electronic index.
- Discuss how call numbers are used to shelve and locate books and other items in the library's physical collection.
- Provide an overview of the library's home page to teach students how and where to access library resources and services.
- Discuss the role of interlibrary loan for acquiring items not available locally.

Understanding/Using Information

Historically, a significant number of instruction requests have been focused on accessing and acquiring information. However, instruction librarians are increasingly being asked to instruct students about all levels of the research process. Among others, they may be as asked to talk about topic development and articulating a specific information need, criteria for evaluating the relative advantages of one source over another, or any of the various moral, legal, and ethical issues surrounding the use of information.

Examples

- Discuss criteria used to evaluate source material for accuracy and relevance.
- Explain the various ways of developing a better research topic or question.
- Describe how to cite an article properly using the APA citation style.

Using Technology

Discussion of various technologies must necessarily be a part of almost any library class. But, like other classes, it may also be taught independently. This type of instruction typically revolves around technical issues and concerns surrounding the research process or the use of library resources and services. But it may also be designed to develop one's familiarity with a specific piece of equipment or software application—in some cases library-specific, and in some cases with broader applications to the research process.

Examples

- Demonstrate how to log in to library resources remotely.
- Show how to use microform equipment.
- Teach how to digitize content for use in other applications (e.g., e-portfolios).
- Provide instruction in the use of PowerPoint to present the results of one's research.

FINDING THE BALANCE

How does one ultimately decide what should be taught? The short answer is that it varies. Some classes may be devoted specifically to a single topic; others incorporate content from two, three, or even all four of the categories outlined above. Determining the specific content for any given class and deciding how much time to devote to each element involve effectively balancing several considerations, including student needs versus teacher expectations, internal versus external goals and objectives, what is known versus what is not known, present versus future needs, breadth versus depth, too much versus not enough time, and transferability versus specificity.

Student Needs vs. Teacher Expectations

It is critical to identify from the start who is requesting the instruction in order to articulate specific needs and expectations for the class. To an extent, it can certainly be argued that "the customer is always right" and that instruction should be geared primarily to those in the class. However, when a professor or someone else requests instruction for a group, instruction librarians need to pay attention to that person's needs and expectations and balance them with those actually taking the class.

When the group self-selects, this process is generally fairly straightforward. The librarian can outline course content, assignments (if any), learning outcomes, and so on for the anticipated participants. In turn, participants know from the start exactly what to expect from the class. Those who feel the class will meet their needs sign up; those more skeptical probably do not.

When instruction is requested on behalf of a group, though, balancing the needs of both students and teacher becomes more problematic. On the one hand, because they are on the front lines, librarians often have firsthand experience helping students overcome the obstacles they face completing their assignments involving the library. As a result, they may have a better grasp of the realities of what instruction students need and can develop a lesson accordingly. On the other hand, instruction librarians need to be cautious about "crossing the line" and providing instruction that was not requested. Just because a librarian perceives or anticipates a student need does not mean she should use a class as her platform to serve that need. She should work with the requestor to ensure that she covers what is desired. Then, as time permits, she can address other topics and issues.

Failure to follow this precept can result in more harm than good. At the very least, it raises questions about the credibility of the library instruction. Agreeing to one thing and then delivering another may make people hesitant about requesting instruction in the future. When they teach what they want rather than what has been requested, instruction librarians also run the risk of appearing uncooperative and selfish. Worse, such librarians may be perceived as uncaring or indifferent to the class, the attending teacher, or both. In some cases, it may even be seen as implying that they do not believe the attending teacher is competent, or that what has been taught is inadequate or inappropriate. In short, although librarians should not refrain from infusing their own perspectives and experiences into the class, they should carefully weigh the potential consequences.

Internal vs. External Goals and Objectives

Instruction librarians should always remember that goals and objectives are tools for accomplishing what is hoped will be achieved with the class. Unfortunately, the terms *goal* and *objective* are often mistakenly used interchangeably. Goals are broad, intangible sorts of ideas that cannot strictly be validated or measured. Objectives, on the other hand, are specific, tangible targets that one sets out to accomplish or measure. Enhancing student research skills, for example, is a typical goal. Developing a workshop that teaches students how to use the library's catalog to find books is an objective.

It is important to recognize that goals and objectives exist at multiple levels. Here, for purposes of discussion, internal goals and objectives are personal or library oriented. Typically these are created by and for the library, employees of the library, and those likely to use the library's resources and services. External goals and objectives are broader in scope and extend beyond the library. They may include such things

GOALS	OBJECTIVES
Broad	Narrow
Ends	Means
General statement of intent	Practical steps needed to reach goal
Generally intangible	Must be tangible
Long-term	Short- or medium-term
Abstract	Concrete
Hard to quantify/measure	Easy to quantify/measure
General direction of action	Specific targets to attain/accomplish
Based on ideas	Based on fact
Cannot be placed on timeline	Should be placed on timeline

as departmental, organizational, institutional, or even societal goals and objectives and are generally outside the ability of the library to modify.

At their respective levels, both internal and external goals and objectives are directed toward the same end, each contributing to and benefiting the other. Broader, external goals and objectives tend to set the stage for the library's internal goals. Conversely, by achieving its internal goals and objectives the library helps the broader institutions meet theirs.

In an ideal world, internal and external goals and objectives coexist and work in alignment. For example, a college may have a goal of expanding its online programs. In turn, a library may have a goal of increasing remote access to library services. An instruction librarian's goal may be to create a course for online students. The goal at each level supports or reflects the goals of the library and the institution or constituencies to which it is responsible.

When internal and external goals and objectives are not in alignment, instruction librarians need to look closely at the instruction they are providing. This is not to suggest that they should discontinue teaching. Sometimes they may be providing instruction to meet a goal or objective not yet identified by the larger community. However, sometimes they may simply be providing instruction to satisfy their own needs and expectations. For example, they may need to keep enrollment numbers up to justify their expenditure of both time and money.

Ultimately, when deciding what to teach, librarians must make every effort to base instruction on some kind of recognized goals and objectives. Certainly the goals of instruction librarians and the library can and should be involved. Gearing instruction to the objectives of class assignments, course syllabi, and course descriptions is also common. But in an age of growing expectations for accountability, matching library instruction goals and objectives to broader institutional ones is increasingly desirable. This provides some measure of accountability. Perhaps more significant, it also helps ensure that the instruction provided by librarians is not self-serving, that it serves a broader, larger audience than just the library or librarians.

What Is Known vs. What Is Not Known

Determining what is already known by students versus what is new or unique content is a significant challenge for every instructor. For obvious reasons, presenting new content is generally preferable to presenting known content; doing the latter risks boring students, creating an atmosphere of indifference, and reducing one's professionalism as an instructor. Yet sometimes familiar content is worth presenting as a form of review and helps ensure that everyone has the same information.

At the root of the problem is the fact that every student comes to class with different levels of experience and expertise with respect to any topic. Although it may seem reasonable to assume that freshmen have less experience using information and conducting research than seniors, there is no guarantee that seniors have such experience or, even if they do, that they are proficient. Even in situations where students take a specific class or course sequence that incorporates research and information skills, it cannot be assumed that all students get the same experience, benefit similarly, or otherwise are information literate or good researchers after this instruction.

This problem is exacerbated by the ever-growing variety of information formats, methods of access, and dependence of information on computer technology. Today's student may be in need of instruction in using computers as much as in conducting research, if not more. Variability in the configuration of computers, browser and other software compatibility issues, and any of a host of other concerns can frustrate even the most savvy of researchers. Worse, many of these challenges are machine-specific: the problem may simply be a temporary, random sort of problem, or a problem associated the specific machine on which they are working. The problem they encounter at home may not be a problem in the library or classroom.

Because of the variability in skills and technologies, it is often difficult to conduct meaningful, individualized assessments of students. There are simply too many variables and considerations to take into account. Nonetheless, either before or during a class, many instructors do rudimentary assessments as a means of determining how much time to spend on a given topic during class. For example, by a simple show of hands or, more recently, by using interactive "clickers," students can indicate if they are comfortable searching the library catalog. If they are, the instructor knows she does not have to spend time on that topic.

However, such assessments pose several challenges on their own. First and foremost, do students know if they are proficient? The way an instructor asks the question can significantly alter the way a student responds. For example, asking "How many feel comfortable using the library's catalog?" is essentially no different than "How many of you have trouble using the catalog?" In both cases, students must assess their own proficiency on the basis of arbitrary and subjective definitions of *comfortable* and *trouble*. A better question might be something like "How long do you spend searching the library's catalog before you find the book you want?" Here, the length of time spent searching is an objective, quantifiable measure.

And yet, quantifying answers does not necessarily solve the problem. First, there are always concerns about the accuracy of self-indicating. On the one hand, students may be hesitant to show their ignorance. Few may willingly admit in front of a group of their peers that they do not know how to do something, particularly if it is something perceived as very basic. On the other hand, they may inflate their knowledge in an attempt to bypass a particular subject or otherwise shorten the class. In fact, if the assessment is done before a class begins, they may indicate proficiency in an attempt to avoid attending class at all.

Equally problematic is determining what constitutes proficiency. Using the above example, a librarian may think that searching a catalog for more than five minutes is excessive. Students, especially those who do not search a catalog often or who lack good information skills, may think that five minutes is reasonable. Either way, this approach fails to take into account other important factors such as the nature of the book being sought or how difficult it is to find it.

Another problem is simply one of numbers. If an instructor is using a hand count to determine whether to cover a topic in class, how many is enough? In a class of twenty-five students, if only two students claim proficiency, most would probably agree that instruction is needed. But what is the magic number? How many students should be proficient before the topic can be bypassed? ten? fifteen? twenty?

Present vs. Future Needs

There are several arguments in favor of focusing content on participants' immediate needs. Librarians usually have a basic understanding of what a teacher expects in terms of an assignment. Sometimes this is because they have worked with the teacher in the creation of the assignment itself. Other times it is because librarians regularly work firsthand with students as they complete their course work. Working with students directly provides librarians with keen insight into the problems students experience at each stage of an assignment. This is especially true for an assignment that has been given in the past.

At the same time, though, this familiarity with the assignment and student needs also enables librarians to look ahead and develop an awareness of challenges students are likely to encounter down the road. Obviously, individual student differences and needs make it impossible to predict and address every possible problem or scenario that may eventually emerge. Often, though, there are general sorts of things that every student is likely to struggle with, and these should be considered when developing course content. For example, a growing number of resources are available electronically from off-site locations. Therefore, it is probably a good idea to at least alert students to the proper procedure for logging in to library resources remotely.

Breadth vs. Depth

Deciding whether to teach more about a few topics or less about more topics is another key content element instructors must consider. Determining how much detail to provide on any given topic depends, to a large extent, on the amount of time available. In a one-hour, one-shot sort of class, the amount of information that can be conveyed is necessarily limited. Some instructors opt to cover as many topics as possible without going into any great detail. Others opt to cover a few topics in depth.

But time is not the only consideration. Instructors must also strive to find an appropriate balance between what is necessary and what is desired. In an introductory class, for example, teaching about the library's catalog is pretty standard and typically involves discussion about such things as basic search strategies and understanding search results. For most beginning researchers, though, learning how to limit by publication place or status would be inappropriate and unnecessarily time consuming.

Along with time, the nature of the content is also relevant to the degree of content specificity to be delivered. Some concepts are simply more difficult to learn. Other topics may simply have multiple layers or aspects and require more time than others to discuss. If not enough detail is provided, students may not learn what they need to know. They may also ask questions, thereby extending the amount of time needed to talk about the topic in class. Likewise, some concepts are best taught via demonstration rather than straight lecture. This often results in spending time doing hands-on activities in class to get the point across.

Sometimes decisions about breadth or depth are not the librarians' to make. A librarian, for example, may not feel it is worthwhile to spend more than a few minutes of class time on a particular topic. The faculty member requesting the instruction, though, may have specific expectations and feel that additional time on the topic is needed.

Too Much vs. Not Enough Time

Every attempt must be made to ensure that the instruction session lasts no longer than it is scheduled to last, but there are several time-related issues that can prevent success in this regard. As outlined earlier, there is almost always more content that *could* be discussed than *can* be discussed within the time allotted. Although this is especially true for one-shot workshops, semesterlong courses suffer from this problem as well. Instructors often need to make tough decisions about what to discuss and for how long simply because there is insufficient time to discuss everything to the desired depth.

For this and other reasons, instructors should always have a well-defined outline of what they plan to present in a class. In drafting this content plan, however, instructors should also have some sense of what can be eliminated as circumstances dictate. For example, most instructors incorporate class time for students to ask questions. The problem that arises, though, is that there is no way to predict how many questions will be asked or how long it will take to answer them. Allotting too much or too little time can leave students and instructors alike feeling frustrated and confused. As a result, being prepared to cut some topics should a class be running long—and having additional, alternative, or anecdotal content to present should a class go too quickly—are always good ideas.

Computer technology can also cause problems with the timing of a class. This is especially true if you must teach in an unfamiliar location with an unexpected hardware configuration or version of the desired software loaded. To reduce or even eliminate delays caused by these sorts of issues, a little bit of preparation goes a long way. Whenever possible, instructors should try any resident technologies a day or two before class to be certain they work. If you cannot do this sort of inspection beforehand, plan to arrive early on the day of class to be sure the desired technologies are available and working properly. At the very least, create copies of files saved in different formats on multiple media. As a rule of thumb, if you are unfamiliar with where you will be teaching, assume the software is at least one version out of date.

Always remember that there are no guarantees. Power outages, network crashes, and a host of other problems may occur with little or no warning. This may mean you have no equipment with which to work. Sluggish or intermittent network connectivity can be particularly frustrating. Although these worst-case scenarios are infrequent, they do occur, and their unpredictability makes them especially troublesome. Like any emergency plan, one hopes it is never used. Still, instructors need to have one so they are prepared to deal with these contingencies if and when they occur.

Transferability vs. Specificity

Transferability is the capacity for something that works in one situation to work in others—in the present context, that what is learned can be transferred to different environments and contexts. An author search for information, for example, is pretty standard across all applications. When an author search is conducted, the results generated are based on finding matching text within the citation's or information record's author field. As result, when individuals conduct an author search, they can expect it to function similarly regardless of the resource being searched.

By contrast, *specificity* is not transferable. As the name suggests, it is a specific, discrete concept unique to a given resource or service. To conduct an author search, one resource might require AU and the name of the author in quotes whereas another resource might require the syntax AUTHOR= and the author's name in quotes. Both resources perform the same search, but the protocol for doing so is different, specific to each of the resources being searched.

When teaching, instructors need to determine how much transferability and specificity to incorporate into the topics being discussed. Transferability generally has a higher degree of abstraction, specificity a higher degree of application. Some find it easier to teach specificity first so as to provide a foundation for higher-level skills and concepts. The danger is that, as contexts and resources change, additional instruction becomes necessary. Others believe that the specifics of any given resource can be figured out if an individual understands the underlying concepts and principles involved. Here, an instructor risks students coming away from a class not knowing how to apply what they have learned.

ASK YOURSELF

Deciding what to teach involves balancing a variety of factors. This can be extremely challenging on numerous levels. But, at the very least, if instruction librarians cannot answer the following questions clearly and succinctly, they really need to take a hard and honest look at the instruction they are providing before deciding to teach a particular course. This is as true for proposed courses as it is for existing, ongoing ones.

> What individual, departmental, library, and institutional goals and objectives will be met by the instruction I am providing?

> How will individual, departmental, library, and institutional goals and objectives for the course be met by my instruction?

> What specific needs and expectations of the assignment, students, teacher, and program will my instruction address? Which will it not address?

> What data do I have that support the instruction I provide? should provide? plan to provide?

SIX WHERE INSTRUCTION TAKES PLACE

ANY MOMENT IS A potential teaching moment. By extension, any place is a potential place of instruction. But what is *place* and how does it impact instruction? Historically, library instruction was limited almost exclusively to the library. This is still the predominant model at many institutions and campuses. Simply put, it involves a designated room or area of the library where instruction occurs. Today, though, it is becoming increasingly common for librarians to provide instruction in locations that are not a part of the library. Among other venues, this may mean visiting a classroom in another building or holding the class in a computer lab. Over the past decade or so, it has also become increasingly common to present instructional elements or even entire courses online. As the number of online courses and programs continues to grow, expectations for remote access to library resources and services are likely to grow as well. As a result, it seems probable that both true online and hybrid models of instruction will occupy a more prominent role in library instruction.

TRADITIONAL VENUES

New things become can familiar quickly these days, so what counts as "traditional" is rather subjective. In the context of library teaching venues, the reference desk, classrooms inside the library and out, computer labs, and the virtual classroom on online instruction are well established.

At the Reference Desk

To varying degrees, an increasing number of reference transactions include an instructional component. As the variety of means of access to and amount of information grow, students are increasingly challenged to know how to search for information effectively. In turn, a growing number come to the reference desk asking about how to use a particular resource. Some librarians are reluctant to provide instruction at the reference desk because it empowers students and takes away from the need for librarians. Others see this empowerment in a positive way that ultimately results in greater credibility of and an even greater need for librarians.

The biggest advantage of using the reference desk as a point of instruction is arguably the face-to-face contact with students. If nothing else, the reference desk provides a common, consistent point of access. The faces may change throughout the day, but the reference desk does not. It remains constant and, as a result, may come to be perceived as the focal point for assistance with library resources and services—not just a place to get quick information or help with research. The reference desk also allows students to interact directly with librarians. When students have a positive experience with a librarian at the desk, that librarian's approachability is increased, as is that of other librarians and the library by association.

Providing instruction at the reference desk can also have negative consequences. Some librarians, for example, may be reluctant to help with what they consider non-traditional reference questions; though not always the case, the majority of questions are often technology-related. The reason for such reluctance varies. Sometimes it is philosophical. The librarian may simply believe such questions are not "reference-worthy" and choose not to try to help. More commonly, though, the hesitation stems from a lack of familiarity with the questioned technology. The librarian simply may not know how to help or may not want to appear foolish by trying. As with any question they have difficulty answering, librarians should refer such students to a person or agency—library-related or not—who may be able to provide assistance. After the fact, it is highly recommended that the librarians work with those expert resources as well so they are better able to answer such questions in the future.

A more significant problem is time. Typically students at the reference desk have a specific question or need. In turn, the answer is specific and focused. Although a librarian can often anticipate additional questions the student may have in the future, there often is not time to provide in-depth or uninterrupted instruction. Even when there is time, some librarians may not see the reference desk as a place to provide instruction, or they may have little desire to teach.

In a Designated Room in the Library

Not surprisingly, teaching within the library has long been the most common venue for library instruction. Typically such instruction takes place in a lab, a designated room for instruction, or some combination thereof. As libraries evolve, more and more have begun using classrooms specifically designed for instructional purposes. Others have designated and outfitted existing space for doing so.

The key advantage to this model is that librarians have control over the space. This makes it much easier to coordinate schedules, manage equipment, and otherwise administer use of the room. In addition, being in the library, it is easier to access. The librarians do not have to pack things up and go somewhere else. It is also a familiar, comfortable location for many and reinforces the idea of using the library.

All of the above have a downside as well. Holding classes in the library, for example, reinforces the notion of "library as place." Because it is not their normal classroom, students may forget or otherwise not know where to go on the day instruction is being provided. In fact, because it is not their classroom or where they normally hold class, teachers may be reluctant to schedule library instruction because of the logistics involved. Even so, unless the classroom is specifically designed for instruction, it may not be instruction-friendly. The computer's projection screen, for example, may be installed in a location that receives a lot of sun, making it difficult to see what is being presented.

In a Nonlibrary Classroom

Sometimes librarians have to teach in a room outside the library. In some cases, a library may simply not have an available classroom in which to provide instruction. There may simply be no room at all, or the room may be scheduled for other purposes. Other times, though, faculty members may request that the librarian come to their classroom. In many cases, the librarian may suggest this as well. This scenario often occurs with longer classes when the teacher plans to continue teaching after the library instruction segment is over.

Because the instruction takes place in their normal room, students do not have to remember where they need to go. They attend class in the same room as their regular class. Meeting them on their turf also demonstrates a high degree of empathy—that the librarian is willing to meet them on their terms, under their conditions. This is a great way to build rapport with students and faculty alike.

However, because the instruction takes place outside the library, the arrangement of the room being used may not suit the librarian's purpose. The furniture and layout of the room may not encourage group work. Transporting materials can be problematic. In the library, a librarian can pull books, journals, and other items from the collection and get them to the classroom fairly easily. When a class is held in a nonlibrary location, the librarian has to determine how best to transport the items, if they are even transportable in the first place. This is even more of a challenge during periods of inclement weather when special care must be taken so things are not damaged in transition.

Similar problems occur with equipment. The room may just not have what is needed to provide instruction. There may not be computers for the students to use. In cases where the proper equipment is available, it may not work or may not work as anticipated. It may also be a different brand or version than that with which the librarian is familiar, requiring time to learn how to use it properly. If a computer is being used, the software may not be loaded, or it may be a different version than that with which the presentation was developed. When teaching in nonlibrary classrooms, librarians should plan to arrive early to check the functionality of the equipment and always have a backup plan ready in case something is not working on the day of instruction.

In a Computer Lab

With so much information being computer-dependent, the need to teach classes in a room with appropriate equipment is almost universal. For that reason, providing instruction in some form of lab is increasingly common and is more the rule than the exception. As with traditional classrooms, the lab may be in the library or in another location. Some labs are designed specifically for instruction. Others are traditional computer labs used for instructional purposes. The latter are often hybrid labs in which the computers are available for general use by students when the lab is not being used to provide instruction.

Clearly the big advantage of teaching in a lab is that such rooms enable librarians to incorporate hands-on, experiential elements into their instruction sessions. Firsthand experience is a well-documented method for improving student learning and retention. Those who are concerned about students using computers for noninstructional purposes during a class may wish to consider using some form of classroom management software. This does not guarantee that the students pay attention, but it ensures that they see only what you want them to see on their computers.

If the lab is a hybrid, though, traffic flow can be an issue. Prior to the start of a class, there may be students doing work in the lab. Someone needs to alert those who are not part of the class that they need to finish what they are doing and exit the lab so that the class can start on time. Even if this is handled tactfully and in a timely manner, it can still generate negative feelings. Posting a schedule of classes several days in advance and giving students ample time to finish up are simple yet highly effective ways to reduce bad feelings before they occur.

Lab usage in general can also be a concern. If the lab is heavily used, some may question the value of holding classes there. This is especially true of small classes and particularly in situations where other workstations are not readily available during classes. Say the lab seats thirty students, and prior to class all thirty workstations are in use. Some might question the relative merit of holding the class over asking the thirty students to leave. They may see this as a misappropriation or underutilization of lab resources, particularly for those classes with small enrollments. For this reason alone, those scheduling a lab for instruction need to weigh seriously the benefits of a class against the benefits of lab use for the students who would be displaced. The acquisition of a cadre of laptops that can be used anywhere is one alternative that should also be considered in place of a standard lab for instruction.

Even for labs that are "pure" (not hybrid), there are common challenges to instruction. For example, on the day of the class, the equipment desired by the librarian may not be available or may not be working. This can be particularly problematic if the lab is not maintained by the library. And even when it is, if the lab is used by multiple instructors, any one of them has the opportunity to change software settings, add/remove applications at will, and otherwise reduce functionality of the workstations used to provide instruction. Beyond that, even if the teaching technology is available and the equipment is operating as expected, there may not be enough computers for the number of students in the class.

Design factors can also be problematic. Many labs are simply not designed for teaching. Students may have difficulty viewing the screen because of too much ambient light or because of the arrangement of the workstations. Bad acoustics can cause problems for students and instructors alike; these sorts of factors can severely compromise the effectiveness of even the best instruction and need to be acknowledged. Doing surveillance of both the lab and the equipment a few days beforehand is always a good idea and goes a long way toward reducing or even eliminating the impact of these sorts of problems.

Online Instruction

Teaching online offers a variety of opportunities for librarians to provide instruction. For example, the instruction can be a complete and self-contained class, or it can be a series of discrete, individual units. The course's pace can be set by the instructor or by the student. It can incorporate documents, files, links, and other items as well as other tools not always available in face-to-face classes. Although the available technology does impose some limits on what can and cannot be done, many of these limits have workarounds or are gradually being eliminated as communication technologies evolve.

Online instruction offers several advantages. Among others, it enables instruction librarians to reach an entirely new audience. Students enrolled in online courses do not come to campus much, if at all. As a result, they are often at a disadvantage in that they never receive face-to-face instruction from a librarian. Providing courses online or developing online instructional materials and programs significantly diminishes this barrier.

Flexibility is also a significant benefit. By their nature, online courses tend to provide greater flexibility in terms of scheduling. The librarian can decide how much time to put into the class and when. Students also generally have greater flexibility about how and when they complete the course work. Assuming a standard platform, course shells and materials can be more readily shared with others who are providing instruction online.

At the same time, the advantages of online instruction can pose significant hurdles. The time needed to develop an online course should not be underestimated. Aside from organizing the course itself, the instruction librarian may need to spend considerable time learning one or more entirely new software applications. Additional time is also needed to convert pen-and-paper items into digital format. Although some of these items can simply be scanned, others (e.g., tests, handouts) may take considerable time and effort to convert. The creation and digitization of completely new items may take even longer. All of this says nothing of the time needed to maintain a course once it becomes available. Verifying links, updating materials, maintaining multiple tests to reduce the possibility of cheating, and similar tasks all need to be done on a regular, ongoing basis.

Course content can quickly become static if the instructor is not involved. True instruction involves more than simply posting and having students navigate through a weekly PowerPoint presentation. Chatting, e-mailing, and otherwise interacting with students online are integral parts of most such courses, but they can be extremely time consuming. Although it is unreasonable to expect an instructor to be available all hours of the day, every day of the week, online students do expect and typically need frequent and regular access to their instructor. Instruction librarians teaching online need to establish a schedule of availability (e.g., "office hours," chat time) and stick to that schedule as much as possible. Alternate scheduling or assignments of librarians may be required to ensure their online availability.

An often overlooked aspect of online instruction is student motivation. As with face-to-face instruction, students are unlikely to enroll in an online course voluntarily, navigate an online tutorial, or otherwise access instructional materials online without some perceived benefit or need. Embedding library instruction in another class and offering some sort of points or course credit for completing the library component are common incentives.

Even so, because a significant part of such instruction is typically self-paced, students enrolled in online courses generally need to be highly motivated, self-starting sorts of individuals. Accordingly, librarians developing online content should make it readily accessible, easy to use, and well organized. Failure in any one of these characteristics may create unnecessary barriers and reduce the value of an otherwise good course or instructional material.

NONTRADITIONAL VENUES

Where we think instruction can or should take place can be based on a variety of factors. For example, when most people think of instruction, they often think of a physical place or specific location (e.g., website), as outlined above. This may be as much based on past experiences as anything. Having a specific, designated location for instruction is what we have all experienced. It is what is familiar to us.

At the same time, how we view where instruction takes place may also be a matter of how we conceive of instruction. Most of us are comfortable defining instruction as a set of activities involving an instructor and students in some sort of structured learning environment. But what about a casual conversation in the parking lot about a library resource? What about a student asking a question in the hallway?

Again, any moment is a potential teaching moment, and therefore any location is potentially suitable for instruction. How broadly or narrowly we define instruction affects how we feel about where instruction takes place. Clearly, though, instruction can take place without a formal classroom or online access point. Unfortunately, many librarians overlook these nonstructured activities as venues for instruction.

Naturally, one would not launch into an hourlong lecture when casually asked what's new at the library. Yet if one thinks about every moment being a potential teaching moment, to overlook these chances to inform others about library resources and services is to overlook a significant instructional opportunity.

Even just getting involved with the lives of those who use the library creates a sense that you are interested in what is going on outside of the library. This is a good way to build rapport and otherwise become better acquainted with those who use or might use the library. Increasing your approachability in this way increases the likelihood of students seeking you out when they do need more formal instruction. The variety of nontraditional venues for instruction is almost unlimited:

- speaking at nonlibrary departmental meetings on behalf of the library
- getting involved with your school's or school district's curriculum committee
- getting involved with other committees and groups at your institution
- making in-service presentations to instructors
- serving as an advisor to a student group
- attending school-sponsored activities (e.g., sporting events) where students and instructors are likely to be present
- having an active presence at events like orientation, alumni weekend, homecoming, and parents' weekend
- maintaining a presence in student publications like the yearbook and newspaper
- working with admissions staff to create an appropriate library script for tour guides
- encouraging and coordinating visits from local K–12 children
- encouraging and coordinating visits from nonschool groups (e.g., senior citizens)
- making contacts with area businesses and organizations that do research
- presenting at institutional workshops and conferences
- interacting with students and faculty in the parking lot, hallway, restroom, bookstore, coffee shop, cafeteria, grocery store
- communicating through library publications—printed and electronic. Always remember that these provide information and teach about the library and should not be produced casually.

Participating in these sorts of activities does not mean teaching. Just being a positive, personable advocate for the library is often sufficient. This means answering questions and participating in discussions—not avoiding questions or discussions because you do not want to be bothered or otherwise are not officially working as a librarian. For that matter, instruction does not have to be about the library. Sometimes simply being approachable and demonstrating that we are interested in them as people (not just as library users) is the best lesson we can give potential library users.

SEVEN IT'S ABOUT TIME

LIBRARIANS NEED TO BE cautious about scheduling instruction for the right, not wrong, reasons. A librarian might schedule instruction simply because he wants to teach a class. Another might do so because she enjoys working with a group or as a favor to the attending teacher. But desirability alone is generally not a sufficient reason. Another common scenario is scheduling instruction simply because it has been requested. In this instance, librarians may fear that failure to provide instruction when requested will reflect negatively on themselves or the library. Such instruction is scheduled more for political reasons than for pedagogical ones.

Before deciding to teach a class, librarians need to take into account a variety of factors and considerations. At the very least, they should try to identify and articulate the specific needs, expectations, and benefits of the class to the possible participants, the associated faculty member, and the library. Doing so clearly helps in developing appropriate course materials and lecture notes. More than that, though, it helps ensure that what the librarian presents, what the attending instructor expects, and what the participants need are all in alignment. Lacking such alignment, library instruction risks becoming busywork. Worse, if the students have difficulty understanding the context of the librarian's instruction, they are unlikely to understand how to apply the concepts and principles presented to their assignments. This wastes everyone's time and can significantly detract from both the library's and the librarian's credibility.

Expressing reluctance to teach is not easy. By their nature, most librarians are service-oriented, with an almost instinctive desire to help. Nonetheless, it is important for them to explain any reluctance to the attending faculty member. Typically, when a librarian expresses reluctance and presents the reasons for it, faculty members are understanding and supportive. Rather than receive no librarian instruction at all, most are willing to work with librarians to ensure that their concerns are adequately addressed and that their students have a meaningful instructional experience.

HOW IS INSTRUCTION INITIATED?

In determining if it is appropriate to provide instruction in the first place, it is important to understand that instruction is typically developed and administered to address a specific need. Credit-bearing classes fall into a distinct category and, for purposes of this discussion, are not covered here. Although they may emerge as a result of or in spite of the following scenarios, I exclude them because they are administered on a regular, ongoing basis. Requests for them need not be initiated; the class is already in place for those wanting to enroll.

In general, stand-alone classes are initiated by potential participants, instructors, the curriculum, or librarians, as follows:

Participant-Initiated

Sometimes individuals request instruction. More often than not, the instruction requested revolves around specific questions or difficulties an individual has experienced as a result of working on a particular assignment or with a technology. Such instruction may also be requested as a follow-up to information presented in another class or venue. For that reason, this type of instruction often takes the form of a workshop in which content is developed to meet the specific needs that have been expressed. Because of its focused nature, this type of instruction often involves one-on-one or small-group sessions.

Instructor-Initiated

An assignment requiring the use of library resources is arguably one of the most common reasons librarians are asked to provide instruction. Here, a faculty member typically contacts a librarian to provide instruction during which the needs and challenges students are likely to encounter in completing an assignment are addressed. To help ensure a professional session and an effective assignment—from both student and faculty perspective—it is important to have a copy of the given assignment well before the actual instruction is to occur. This allows adequate time for the instructing librarian to prepare for the session, ask questions about the content or focus of the assignment, and so on.

Sometimes, though, instructors simply want to expose their students to what the library has to offer. These instruction sessions are usually more awareness-heightening activities than formalized instruction; rather than explaining how to do something, the emphasis is on simply making students aware of available resources and services. Tours and scavenger hunts are two examples of this sort of instruction.

Curriculum-Initiated

Curriculum-initiated instruction is instituted because of some expressed need or concern at the institution or community level. Accreditation requirements are a common catalyst for such courses. For example, a university may be asked to have a stronger research component embedded into a particular department or even into the overall general education component of its curriculum. Credit-bearing classes often fall under this category.

Other times, such courses are developed as part of a "student success program" or as a means of providing deeper coverage of topics and concepts than can be provided in a one-shot, workshop type of class. These courses are often credit-bearing and may be offered independently by the library or as part of another department's curriculum.

Librarian-Initiated

Here, a librarian initiates the need for instruction directly. For example, perhaps a librarian has noticed that students are having trouble completing a particular assignment. She might then contact the professor, suggesting an instruction session geared toward addressing the problems she has encountered. Other times, a librarian may notice that many students are repeatedly asking the same questions or experiencing the same problems. For example, perhaps they do not cite sources properly. The librarian might then develop an open workshop that students can attend to learn how to cite sources.

WHEN SHOULD INSTRUCTION BE SCHEDULED?

Once a decision has been made to provide instruction, it is time to consider scheduling options. When one is scheduling any given instruction session, the following key time-related elements should be considered:

Ensuring Librarian Availability

Whatever method is used to assign responsibilities for instruction, obviously a librarian needs to be available to be scheduled for that instruction. Often overlooked here is a clear idea of what happens if that librarian is unable to provide instruction as scheduled because of illness or some other reason. Sometimes others are able and available to fill in. Other times the class needs to be canceled. Having a policy or procedure in place can go a long way toward avoiding additional complications now and in the future. At the very least, when faculty members are involved, every attempt should be made to contact them as quickly as possible to alert them to the problem and to determine if and how they wish to proceed.

Specifying a Date/Time

The specific time a class can be offered may or may not be up to the librarian. For example, in credit-bearing classes the course meets on assigned days at a specific time as established by the department or institution. There is often little flexibility; the class is simply offered when it is offered. The scheduling of one-shot types of classes is generally far more flexible in that they are scheduled only one time and are dependent only upon coordinating a single, specific day and time to hold the instruction.

The scheduling of independent instruction—instruction created and administered solely at the discretion of the library—has the flexibility of being offered at any time on any day. In such instances, librarians need to balance personal needs and wants with those of the class. For example, although a morning person might want to schedule a class at 8 a.m., those who might participate may find this is too early and not attend, or they may attend but pay less attention than if the class was later in the day.

For public and some specialized libraries, attention needs to be paid to traffic flow. Because of family, occupational, or other commitments, users of these libraries may not be able to attend a class offered during the standard nine-to-five workday. Evening or weekend classes are often a far better fit for these individuals.

Recognizing Schedule Density

Instructors need to keep in mind that some times during the day are more heavily scheduled than others. At a university, for example, there are likely to be far more classes scheduled between, say, 10 a.m. and 2 p.m. than at other times. This does not mean that scheduling a class during this period is inappropriate, but instructors should be aware that attendance may be less because of competition with other classes. At the same time, less dense time slots are not necessarily better. Although students may have greater flexibility to take an 8 a.m. class, they may not have the motivation to do so. Likewise, although it might seem that people are more available during the lunch or dinner hour, this is also when people eat, run errands, and perform other personal tasks.

Being Aware of School and Community Calendars

When scheduling classes, pay attention to the school and community calendars. There may be events scheduled on a daily, weekly, or monthly basis that make scheduling instruction problematic. Guest speakers, athletic events, and student or faculty meetings are good examples. Although most of these are optional, some events may be required as part of a project or class. Obviously, if an instruction session is scheduled during a time when one of these activities is scheduled, the population of available students is diminished accordingly.

Time-Related Ergonomic Considerations

In considering when a class is to be taught, two key ergonomic considerations are often overlooked. For one, it may be difficult for students and librarian to view a video presentation at certain times because of the angle and brightness of the sun. Even with the lights off and blinds drawn, there may still be too much ambient light to view things properly. Similarly, it may also be hard to hear during certain times of the day, such as if there is construction going on nearby, regular distractions in the hallway, and so on.

Another concern is seating. A previous class in the room may have used a different seating arrangement. As a result, a librarian may need to spend time at the start of class aligning chairs, desks, and other furniture, particularly if the room is in another department or a building other than the library. Librarians should prepare to arrive early for the duration of the course or consider changing to an alternate location if spending time on these tasks uses up too much class time.

Personal Time Considerations

We all have times when we are more alert, more focused, and otherwise better able to perform more effectively than at other times. Simply put, some of us are morning people, others are night owls. Translated? If you are most alert and energetic at 9 a.m., it is probably better to schedule classes as close to then as possible rather than at eight o'clock at night. By being aware of your own natural rhythms, you will be far more effective as an instructor. You will also be far happier in the long run, as will your students.

DEVELOPING AND ADMINISTERING INSTRUCTION

Some instruction takes more time to develop. The same is true for administering instruction. Developing and then teaching a credit-bearing course, for example, obviously requires a huge commitment of time, especially the first time the course is taught. But even planning and conducting a one-shot instruction session can be more time consuming than you might think.

Regardless of the format and medium of the class, presenting the class itself is relatively straightforward if you have done a good job preparing beforehand. Still, effective instructors know that most classes do not (and should not) end when the class is over. Once instruction has been provided, students are typically more likely to seek out the librarian who worked with or taught their class than to seek assistance from other librarians. They may need to follow up on the details of using a specific resource or have other questions that either were not addressed during the instruction

session or arose later. Either way, there are several pre- and post-instruction considerations to keep in mind while budgeting your time:

- deciding how long the class will run
- deciding how much time to devote to each part/element of the class
- determining if there will be an opportunity for a follow-up session
- deciding whether to schedule alternate days/times prior to the class or only as the need arises
- reserving the appropriate room and equipment
- developing lecture notes, assignments, and other class materials
- collaborating with the faculty member to address specific assignment needs and to ensure a meaningful assignment
- completing support tasks (e.g., photocopying handouts)
- conducting a pre- or post-assessment
- offering individualized follow-up assistance as needed
- alerting colleagues to the assignment and what the faculty member expects from students

ONLINE OR FACE-TO-FACE?

Although the situation is changing, direct delivery of instruction has been and continues to be the primary mode of instruction. As a result, those who must learn how
to teach on the job have a context for developing and administering instruction. Even
if they have never done so themselves, they are at least familiar with the process for
developing handouts and other course materials. For most, it is a fairly straightforward process to translate personal classroom experiences into one's own class and
method of instruction.

With indirect methods of instruction such as online courses, this is not necessarily the case. Among other factors, instructors generally need a working knowledge
of numerous software applications and concepts. Adding to this problem is the fact
that the greater degree of interactivity among online students and their instructor
typically places unique demands on an instructor's time, more so than many people
realize. Here are three of the most significant demands:

Learning Technology

Potential instructors need to be aware that there is an implicit learning curve with
most technologies and applications used to place a class online. Those wishing to
teach online need to determine how much time it will take them to make the transition to the online environment. Software changes all the time, and what was used
even two or three years ago may be dramatically different or even unavailable today.
And allocating time to learn new software alone is generally not enough. Many
instructors overlook the time it takes to digitize files and place them online. In fact,

many items digitized in one format may now need to be redigitized—perhaps even in multiple formats—to be more compatible with newer technologies and devices. Additional time is also needed to organize the files in a meaningful way once they are posted as well as alter or remove them when they are no longer appropriate.

Time and Timeliness of Interaction

If the librarian is to be embedded in the course and working with students, time needs to be allocated for participation in things such as online discussion forums. This commitment can be significant or minimal. It seems misplaced to incorporate a chat function into a course and then not be available to participate in it, but the amount of time required is often underestimated. Therefore, from the start, online instructors are strongly encouraged to articulate clearly to their students both the amount of time and the times they will be available to chat.

As an online instructor, you need to articulate when, how, and how often you are going to interact with your students. In a face-to-face class you have a known, prescribed time for the class. In the online world, the class is essentially held all day long unless specified otherwise. For example, without clear guidelines and parameters (e.g., that you will be online nine to midnight each evening for a live chat), some students may send you a chat request at two in the morning. You are certainly not expected to be awake and involved with your students 24/7, but there is a reasonable expectation that you are regularly and frequently monitoring what is going on.

Time Spent per Student

Working with students in an online course can be far more time consuming than working with the same number of students in a face-to-face version of the same course. As a simple example, think of a face-to-face class of twenty-five students that meets every day. Let's say you have five questions in a typical hourlong class and you spend five minutes responding to each question. That results in a little over two hours

TIME-SAVING SUGGESTIONS FOR ONLINE COURSES

- Address questions in the order they are received.
- Clearly articulate when you will be online to chat with students.
- Post clear information about when items will be posted and when removed. Be especially clear about when grades and other forms of feedback will become available and when they will go offline (if at all).
- Work to ensure that any and all comments focus on the course or course content.
- Develop support materials to which students can be referred rather than repeat the same information to multiple individuals.
- Suggest that students include class name and nature of question in the subject line of e-mailed messages, particularly if you are teaching more than one class at a time.

per week spent addressing questions. In the same class taught online, you may have all twenty-five students asking questions, many more than once in the same 24-hour period. Even if you interact with each student just five minutes per day, that is more than ten hours per week just responding to questions.

Exacerbating the issue is the fact that questions in online classes are often not straightforward. The initial question may seem innocent and simple; for example, a student might start by asking what resource to use to begin a research project. But this can quickly lead to questions about what terms to use, what strategy to employ, and more.

PROCESSING REQUESTS FOR INSTRUCTION

It is highly recommended that instruction librarians provide students and classroom instructors with an organized, consistent means for requesting instruction. Verbal requests are simply not reliable; librarians and instructors alike may forget the details discussed. Moreover, such information typically needs to be transcribed into some form of printed or electronic record-keeping system. There are six primary steps to consider when processing requests for instruction.

Step 1: Identify Who Will Coordinate Requests for Instruction

Depending on how librarians are assigned to teach a course, there may be one or more individuals responsible for scheduling instruction. If there is more than one, this may create an unnecessary layer of confusion. For example, the librarian assigned to a class checks the calendar and determines that the classroom is not available on the requested date but that it is a week later. He promptly calls the classroom instructor to ask if the alternate date would be acceptable. Unfortunately, by the time he speaks with the instructor and confirms the date, he discovers that a colleague has already scheduled the classroom for that time.

Having a single individual responsible for processing instruction requests virtually eliminates this problem and can greatly streamline the process. But it is not without its own challenges. If this duty is assigned to a librarian, for example, it necessarily takes time away from other duties, including preparing for and teaching classes. If the duty is assigned to a nonlibrarian, that individual may not know the answers to questions as well as someone who actually provides instruction.

Step 2: Create a "Request for Instruction" Form

To expedite the gathering of all necessary scheduling information and to avoid having to contact the requester multiple times, most instruction librarians employ some form of standardized instruction request form. Such forms can be either printed or electronic. The latter incorporate greater functionality than a printed form, but the librarian's ability to obtain or use the software for creating them may be prohibitive. See the sidebar "Class Request Forms" for samples from other institutions.

What information is to be supplied on a Request for Instruction form depends on what information is deemed necessary by the library or librarian to whom the request is being directed. There also may be some variation depending on whether the form is in printed or electronic format. At the very least, the form should include the information necessary to facilitate the scheduling and administration of the class. Figure 7.1 is a sample online Request for Instruction form; it is not exhaustive or relevant in detail to all libraries. Figure 7.2 provides an overview of the information requested on the form.

Step 3: Clearly Articulate Specific Rules, Conditions, and Expectations

As part of or in addition to the actual instruction request form, instructors and students need to know what rules (if any) are in place with respect to scheduling instruction. For example, are there prerequisite skills or knowledge that students are expected to have prior to class? Although such information is important, care should be exercised with how this information is presented so that you do not sound aloof or condescending. To help avoid bad feelings, consider adding context or explanation for some items, such as the following:

- Make instructors aware of time limits for topics. It is impossible to cover every topic in any given class. But people requesting instruction may not know how long it takes to discuss a particular topic. Providing guidelines helps instructors and librarians alike to decide what to talk about during a class. Example: "Finding books—15 minutes."
- Provide objectives and specific topics for content. Along with time limits, this significantly aids in the planning process. Example: "Students will

---

SAMPLE CLASS REQUEST FORMS

Baylor University, www.baylor.edu/lib/rli/index.php?id=30424

University of California–Berkeley, www.lib.berkeley.edu/instruct/classrequestform_session.html

Indiana University–Bloomington, www.indiana.edu/~libinstr/instruction/form13.html

Ohio State University–Mansfield, http://library.mansfield.ohio-state.edu/userguides/instruction-form.cfm

Phoenix College, www.pc.maricopa.edu/departments/library/forms/instructrequest.html

Rio Hondo College, http://library.riohondo.edu/About_The_Library/ScheduleOrientation1.htm

Washburn University, www.washburn.edu/mabee/services/instructreq.shtml

FIGURE 7.1   EXAMPLE OF AN ONLINE "REQUEST FOR INSTRUCTION" FORM

XYZ LIBRARY INSTRUCTION REQUEST FORM

For additional information about instructional opportunities in the library or about creating effective library assignments, please visit our "User Education" web page (www.reqform .school.edu) or contact Prof. John Doe (321-555-7654; jdoe@email.edu).

STEP 1: Instructor Information

Date Request Submitted_____Your Name _____

Phone _____ ext. _____ E-mail _____

STEP 2: Course for Which You Are Requesting Instruction

Course Number (e.g., MATH104)_____ Number of Students _____

Course Title (e.g., Finite Math)_____

Preferred Location

☐   Library _____ Room _____

☐   Building _____ Room _____

STEP 3: Scheduling Information

Requests are scheduled in the order they are received. However, it is not always possible to schedule everyone's first preference, so please include an alternate choice.

1st Preference

Day _____Date _____ Start_____ am/pm Stop _____ am/pm

2nd Preference

In case we cannot schedule you for your first preference, please list an alternate choice.

Day _____ Date_____ Start_____ am/pm Stop _____ am/pm

Do you have a preference for a librarian? If so, please indicate his/her name.

1st Choice _____ 2nd Choice _____

STEP 4: Assignment Information

Please attach a copy of your assignment when you submit your request. Instruction will not be scheduled until the librarian assigned to work with your students has had a chance to review the assignment. If you do not have an assignment or would like feedback on your assignment, please contact Prof. J. Doe (321-555-7654; jdoe@email.edu).

Attach File

STEP 5: Presentation Desired

Library instruction is based on and geared toward research assignments. Please click on the "Read/Hide Description" link for more details on the instruction option(s) that interest(s) you. For topics not listed or to develop a more customized instruction session, please discuss your needs with the librarian working with your class. For single-class sessions, instruction is primarily lecture-based. For more detailed instruction or additional hands-on experience, please schedule additional sessions. The times suggested below should be considered minimums. Please select up to 40 minutes for a 50-minute class (60 minutes for 75-minute classes). Any remaining time will be spent on basic computing issues and questions/answers.

Required

☐ Time for Questions/Answers (5–10 minutes)

Optional (please check all that apply)

Note: All times reflect 5–10 minutes per class for questions and answers. You will not be able to submit a form whose content exceeds the class time you have indicated above.

☐ Finding Books (10–15 mins.) **Read/Hide Description**

☐ Finding Articles (20–25 mins.) **Read/Hide Description**

☐ Searching the Internet (20–25 mins.) **Read/Hide Description**

☐ Using RefWorks (15–20 mins.) **Read/Hide Description**

SUBMITTING YOUR REQUEST

Part A

You must read and agree to the Guidelines for Library Instruction.

☐ I have read and agree to the Guidelines for Library Instruction.

Guidelines

Part B

When submitting your request, you *must* enter an active campus e-mail address as your username (e.g., jd091234@ university.edu).

Submit

FIGURE 7.2   EXPLAINING THE "REQUEST FOR INSTRUCTION" FORM

Introduction. Because not everyone will obtain this page in the same way, it is always good to start off with the name of your library, a contact person/information, and a description of what the page is to be used for. Whatever is included here, keep it brief.

Step 1: Instructor Information. Information needed to contact the individual requesting the instruction.

- The "Date Request Submitted" space enables the ordering of requests based on the date on which they are received.
- Although not necessary, requesting the individual's department affiliation is helpful for record-keeping purposes and in the rare instance when two people with the same name submit a request. In the form, this information is usually implicit in the course number, but it could also be requested separately.

Step 2: Course for Which You Are Requesting Instruction. Information about the course and the number of students expected.

- This section is more for record-keeping purposes than anything. Each library must decide what specific information it wants to record.
- For planning and other purposes, it is important to know how many students are in the class.
- Some may want the instruction to take place in a location other than the library.

Step 3: Scheduling Information. Information needed to schedule the class.

- Include any scheduling issues/procedures (e.g., scheduled in order received).
- What information a librarian needs to schedule instruction will determine what information is requested here. What is indicated is the minimum.
- Alternate date and time information is not necessary. However, it can save a lot of time and effort (e.g., phone calls, e-mails) in the long run if this information is available at the time of the request.
- Depending on how librarians are scheduled, you may want to include a section asking about alternate librarians to provide instruction.

Step 4: Assignment Information. Information about the assignment or the reason the class is being scheduled.

- Not every library requires a review of an assignment before instruction is scheduled. However, requiring a copy of the actual assignment helps ensure that both the librarian and the classroom teacher are in alignment with what is expected. It also adds a measure of credibility to the library's instruction program and virtually eliminates requests for "babysitting" (e.g., the instructor just wants someone to be with his class while he is away for the day).
- Having a copy of the assignment beforehand also gives the instruction librarian a chance to ask questions, point out potential problems, and so on before class. This is particularly helpful when developing a lesson plan for a class for the first time or for the first time a librarian works with a particular class, assignment, or instructor.
- For term projects, a list of topics students are researching can also be very helpful.

Step 5: Presentation Desired. Specific information about what the classroom faculty member would like to have taught to his students.

- Let requesters know if times and content are relative or absolute.
- Because many faculty members are not aware of the time it takes to cover some topics, it is important to include an overview of what can be covered and to give a sense of how long that will take.

- For web forms, preventing someone from scheduling more instruction than the time allotted is highly recommended. No one should be allowed to submit the form for 90 minutes of instruction for a class that is only an hour long.
- Elements (e.g., basic computing, Q&A) that are part of every class should be indicated or at least anticipated.
- When possible, a read/hide link to the content/description for each topic is helpful and prevents the form from becoming unnecessarily long. For example, the description for "Finding Books" might read: *Discussion of the library's catalog— FINDIT—revolves around a simple keyword search for books and other items owned by the library followed by a brief discussion of availability, call numbers, and item locations.*

Submitting the Request

Part A: Rules/Guidelines. Specific rules and guidelines about submitting the form and/or library instruction.
- There are advantages and disadvantages to having this information at the beginning or at the end of the form.
- Placing a copy here of any guidelines, rules, and so on about scheduling instruction helps reduce confusion and frustration. In our sample form, for example, there is a link to guidelines.
- Be specific but be brief. Having this information hidden/revealed at the user's discretion can be particularly helpful in this regard so as not to "clutter" the form. Some sample guidelines to consider:
  - Instruction will not begin until both the librarian and the instructor are present.
  - Instruction must be scheduled at least one week in advance and is geared to XYZ students, faculty, and staff. Instruction for non-XYZ groups and individuals will be provided as time and staffing permit.
  - Classes involving research assignments are given priority. Instruction for classes involving nonresearch assignments will be scheduled as space and librarian availability permit.
  - You will receive confirmation once your class has been scheduled.
  - Please submit one form per class requested.

Part B: Authentication. Instructions, if any, for supplying authentication information.
- Some libraries may restrict instruction to particular groups of people (e.g., current students). Requiring authentication information means that *only* those with the proper credentials can submit a request.

Submit Button

Link this button to the e-mail address to which this form is to be directed. This might be a specific person (e.g., secretary, head of instruction) or group of people (e.g., all those providing library instruction). The individuals to whom this is linked need to be aware that they will be receiving such messages/requests. Consider having the form "repopulate" certain information (e.g., contact, content requested) for individuals requesting multiple classes.

learn how the Library of Congress Classification system is used to arrange books in the collection."

- Requests must be received at least one week in advance. This allows instructors time to tell their students about when and where to meet and you time to plan your lesson, review assignments, and so on.
- Incomplete forms/requests will delay processing of the request. This goes without saying, but following up to determine what date or time a person wants to schedule a class can be more time consuming than you might think.
- Class will not be held unless the professor attends with the class. Students often have questions about their assignment that the librarian cannot answer. Having the classroom faculty member present has several benefits including adding a layer of credibility and aiding in classroom manage-ment.

Step 4: Decide How to Handle Requests Not to Schedule a Particular Librarian

Sometimes certain instructors request that a particular librarian not be assigned to teach their classes. The reasons for such a request can range from a bad experience in the past to a simple conflict of personalities. Whatever the reason, though, this makes scheduling instruction problematic, particularly if the person doing the scheduling is the librarian with whom the instructor has issues.

There is not necessarily an easy way to resolve such situations. Obviously, dis-cussing the problem and attempting to address it is a good idea. However, this often places both the librarian and the faculty member in an awkward position. For small libraries that have only one person providing instruction, the professor may prefer to no longer request instruction rather than deal with the person with whom he has had a problem in the past. Once the problem has surfaced, one possibility is to have a neutral party do the scheduling (e.g., department secretary) and ask everyone request-ing instruction if they have a preference for one instruction librarian. Again, though, some instructors may simply not schedule a class rather than go through the awk-wardness of scheduling a class with a librarian with whom they are uncomfortable.

Step 5: Maintain a Public Calendar

When scheduling classes, it is highly recommended that you record them on a read-ily available, publicly accessible calendar. Such a calendar alerts colleagues (e.g., reference and circulation desks) as to when extra bodies might be in the library. It also alerts individuals to the availability of the classroom. At the very least, if the classroom can be used by others when not being used to provide library instruction (e.g., computer lab), a sign posted outside the door alerting potential users about classes is a good idea.

In addition to obvious administrative and record-keeping value, having a single, accessible calendar has several other advantages. It alerts others to when classes are being held and thus is a good way to advertise instructional opportunities and draw attention to the library. A common calendar also helps avoid cross-scheduling the classroom/lab and provides others with a means to determine when a librarian might (or might not) be available.

Printed calendars are familiar and easy to maintain. Since they can be as simple as a printed word processing document, there is little to no training involved. Unfortunately, printed calendars can be damaged, removed, or altered. They can also be changed without anyone's notice. They are prone to typographical and inputting errors, and the person responsible for maintaining such a calendar may forget to post it or post the incorrect dates and times.

Electronic calendars virtually eliminate several of these errors. They are always current, for the information is updated as soon as it is entered. They are generally accessible via any computer with Internet access. On the downside, as with a printed calendar, the person entering the data may mistype or enter the information incorrectly. And even if it is entered correctly, individuals may still have difficulty locating and accessing the calendar or may not have access to a computer to do so.

Step 6: Inform Students and the Classroom Teacher if You Cannot Teach a Class

Occasionally illness, transportation problems, or family emergencies prevent a librarian from teaching a scheduled class. In such instances, each library must decide if having another librarian substitute is advisable. Any substitute is more likely to be unfamiliar with the class and what is expected. Substitutes may not have time to prepare handouts or lecture notes. They may not be familiar with the content to be discussed or be aware of what has already been discussed in previous classes. Even so, considerable class time might pass while trying to find someone to cover the class, particularly if the librarian has to travel to another building.

If at all possible, the librarian providing the instruction should alert the appropriate person in the library about being unable to teach the class. That person can then go to the classroom and alert the instructor and students that the class must be rescheduled. If the classroom is in another building, contacting the department or area secretary is strongly recommended. Obviously there may be times when contact is impossible. Except in those situations, though, failure to make the attempt to contact someone can be far more damaging in the long run than having a few students show up who did not get the message.

A FINAL WORD ON SCHEDULING

In deciding if a class is worth teaching and, if so, when, instructors need to remember that declining a request for instruction is always an option. Such a decision may be an uncomfortable or even unpopular one, but sometimes it is the right decision and needs to be made. Ultimately, deciding whether or not to provide instruction is and should be the responsibility of the librarian asked to provide instruction.

There are any of a number of reasons to turn down a request for instruction, or at least to delay scheduling it. Among others, particularly in times of reduced budgets, resources, and staff, there may simply not be anyone available to teach at the requested time. Although many librarians bend over backward to change their schedule and responsibilities to accommodate a class, this suggests that librarians' time and work are less valuable than those of the individual requesting instruction. And all of this says nothing about those librarians who *are* available but are not interested or lack the experience to provide instruction; scheduling such individuals may cause more problems than it solves.

Another good reason to delay or not schedule instruction is an ineffective assignment. On one level, the assignment could simply be poorly designed. Among other problems, the required resources might not be available or the wordings and expectations of various assignment elements may be unclear. On an even simpler level, the assignment may simply not have been shared with the librarian asked to provide the instruction. In both cases, developing effective instruction is problematic, to say the least. Asking that the faculty member share her assignment with the librarian well in advance of the instruction session helps avoid these and similar problems.

EIGHT CHARACTERISTICS OF EFFECTIVE INSTRUCTORS

EFFECTIVE INSTRUCTION: HOW MUCH is it mastery of skills and teaching techniques, how much one's attitude toward the work? Can any individual become an effective instructor, or is there an inherent set of qualities or unique disposition that some people possess and others do not? On this continuum, most instructors fall somewhere in between. At one end, having the appropriate credentials, training, and experiences does not necessarily mean an individual is an effective teacher. At the other, although the desire to be an effective instructor is certainly important, attitude and desire alone provide no guarantees to success either.

An equally important continuum is the degree that the instruction itself contributes to the overall effectiveness of a class. Can instruction be effective regardless of who is providing it? It is easy to see how inappropriate content or the illogical structuring of a class can derail even the most effective of instructors. But, at the other end, if a well-planned, well-constructed lesson is administered by someone with no teaching experience or poor presentation skills, can the instruction still be effective?

It helpful to note that *every* learning situation—regardless of the context—involves an instructor and a lesson, and that each of these dimensions can be either effective or ineffective. The instructional scenario matrix below schematizes the interaction between these qualitative elements. Although this oversimplification does not answer the questions posed above, it does provide a framework for understanding the possible answers.

Scenario A: This is the best-case scenario. Both the instructor and the instruction provided are positively aligned to create an effective learning environment. Among other things, content is presented in an upbeat, enthusiastic, and supportive manner that meets the goals, needs, and expectations of the participants, course, program, or institution. Similarly, the instruction is creative and engaging and incorporates a variety of instructional methods to help ensure that everyone has a chance to learn.

Scenario B: The assumption here is that anyone can be an effective instructor if the lesson is well designed. Those not familiar with teaching or education often fall into this category. Many naively assume that teaching is merely a matter of presenting content. But even those who are more familiar with instruction mistakenly believe that, if the instruction is sufficiently well developed and organized, anyone can administer it successfully.

	EFFECTIVE LESSON	INEFFECTIVE LESSON
Effective instructor	A	C
Ineffective instructor	B	D

Scenario C: This is the reverse of scenario B. The assumption is that even bad instruction can be made good with the right person, that somehow a good teacher will know what to do and adjust the instruction accordingly. Charisma, enthusiasm, creativity, and similar traits are seen as enabling one to compensate for or overcome any shortcomings of the content or organization of the instruction itself.

Scenario D: No one wins in this worst-case scenario. The presentation is not effective and the instructor is not good at teaching. In many (most?) situations when this occurs, it might be better to provide no instruction at all. Aside from failing to achieve instructional goals and objectives, what is often overlooked is the intangible impact this scenario has on the perceived value and credibility of both the librarian and the library.

CREATING A POSITIVE LEARNING ENVIRONMENT

The first step in becoming an effective instructor is creating an effective, positive learning environment. The degree to which instructors succeed in this relates directly to their success as instructors. Such an environment not only benefits the students but also is a good way to build upon and strengthen an instruction program. Elements that constitute such an atmosphere include the following:

- Being prepared. Being prepared. Being prepared.
- Giving everyone who wants to teach an opportunity to do so and scheduling those who do not want to teach as little as possible. Desire obviously does not equal quality. Students do, however, tend to recognize and respond better to those instructors who are enthusiastic and have a genuine desire to be in the classroom.
- Incorporating a variety of techniques, examples, learning activities, and other strategies as a means of engaging every member of the class.

- Teachers infusing value with their presence. What value does your presence add to the class? Effective instructors do more than simply read their lecture notes verbatim or present their slides. If students can do just as well simply reading your notes or viewing your presentation, you are not *teaching*.
- Always remembering that the instruction is for the student. You may want to demonstrate all of the library's newest resources and discuss its various services, but this is not necessarily appropriate. Instructors need to respect the needs and expectations of the class and attending instructor and administer instruction accordingly.
- Presenting the same instruction to multiple groups as consistently as possible. Although there are some disadvantages, standardized instruction helps ensure that key points and concepts are presented. It also significantly alleviates the burden of preparing separate materials, lecture notes, and so on for every class.
- Paying attention to questions/problems you experience. This not only builds rapport but can help you modify lectures, handouts, and so on for subsequent classes.
- Constantly striving to develop good, effective assignments and revisiting them on a regular basis for relevance and accuracy.
- *Always* relating instruction to an assignment or some clearly articulated standard or need.

TWENTY-FIVE CHARACTERISTICS OF EFFECTIVE INSTRUCTORS

Many position announcements are based on one form or another of the ACRL Standards for Proficiencies for Instruction Librarians and Coordinators of June 2007, which emerged out of a need to identify and define core skills and proficiencies for instruction librarians as well as instruction coordinators. These skills and proficiencies are grouped into twelve broad skill and knowledge categories:

administrative	leadership
assessment and evaluation	planning
communication	presentation
curriculum knowledge	promotion
information literacy integration	subject expertise
instructional design	teaching

So what exactly constitutes effective instruction? The answer to this question is often subjective. Most of us can look back and easily recall a good teacher or class. Unfortunately, it is often just as easy to remember a bad teacher or class. In either case, though, it may be difficult to articulate what specifically made the teacher or class good or bad.

That said, there are some generally recognized elements that constitute good, effective instruction. The remainder of this chapter summarizes these concepts along broad themes and ideas; this is in no way intended to be exhaustive or prioritized. Someone may *not* possess all of these characteristics and yet still be a good teacher. Some of these characteristics can be developed, others are closer to being simply innate—you either have it or you don't. However they come by them, effective instructors have them:

Knowledge of the subject matter. The more you know about what you are intending to teach, the more confident you are and the more credible you appear. Knowledge of the subject matter also gives you more confidence to answer questions or to address situations that might arise during an instruction session.

Genuine desire to teach. Everyone has off days. But if you do not care about what you are teaching, how can you expect students to care? Students know when someone does not want to teach or is bored, intimidated, or otherwise not interested in teaching. A positive, enthusiastic instructor can go a long way toward helping students stay focused and become engaged in the learning process—in the classroom and beyond.

Knowledge of effective teaching and pedagogy. Traditionally, librarians have had little training in providing instruction. Many have learned to do what they do through on-the-job experiences. For these individuals especially, the value of taking a class on curriculum development, teaching methods, and similar education- or instruction-related courses cannot be overrated. However instructors acquire their training, it is important that they regularly participate in ongoing professional development opportunities.

Engagement with their lessons. Effective instructors are constantly seeking ways to revise and otherwise improve the instruction they provide. Doing so on a regular basis demonstrates your commitment to your class and your students. Two easy things you can do are (a) modify how you present material, and (b) inspect your handouts, notes, and other presentation materials on a regular basis for dated, incorrect, and other inappropriate information. Failure to be actively involved with your lessons can be seen as evidence of a lack of professionalism, laziness, or worse.

Rapport with students and colleagues. Establishing rapport helps keep students engaged, facilitates learning, and generates positive feelings for students and instructors alike. There are any of a number of techniques for establishing rapport. Being available and accessible to students and other instructors alike is certainly a key element. Some others include having personal boundaries, showing respect, demonstrating empathy, accepting students for themselves, and being honest with students.

Fairness. There truly are no "stupid questions." The reality is that everyone has different levels of understanding, different expectations, and different needs. Because of this, it is imperative that instructors respond to each student with appropriate levels and amounts of attention. This is even more important when students are being evaluated. Instructors need to work to ensure that they treat all students equally and fairly.

Flexibility. No matter how many times you have rehearsed a presentation, rarely a class goes by that an instructor is not called upon to change something; for example, one class may ask a lot of questions, forcing you to either eliminate certain topics in your presentation or reduce the amount of time you spend on them. Instructors, though, also need to be flexible outside of the classroom; for example, they may be called upon by a faculty member to change an assignment based on emergent or specialized needs within a particular student population.

High expectations of their students. Students typically do more and do better if they are expected to do so from the beginning. It is difficult to raise the bar midstream—far easier to set high expectations from the start and lower them later if circumstances dictate. In setting expectations, be careful not to set the bar too high, which can frustrate everyone and present a serious challenge to learning.

Openness to criticism. Instructors need to be open to critiques of their work and of their instruction. For example, rather than simply give a student a score he earns, some instructors eliminate questions that more than a specified percentage of a class miss. The idea is that the problem is not with the student but with the instructor. Clearly, students' grades should not be reduced because the instructor does not adequately cover the material, provides incorrect or misleading information, or does not phrase a question in a way that students can understand.

Ability to communicate effectively. Effective communication is imperative if instruction is to be successful. This is certainly important in the classroom. But working with faculty members both before and after class to develop assignments and share insights about information needs from a librarian's perspective are also critical. Keep in mind as well that communication is not just verbal communication. Learning to communicate effectively in written, multimedia, and other formats only increases one's effectiveness as an instructor.

Emphasis on positive reinforcement. It is well documented that positive reinforcement is far more effective than negative reinforcement. Offering encouragement, accepting students at their level, rewarding and acknowledging accomplishments, and helping them set goals and achieve them are all great ways of reinforcing and, ultimately, generating positive results.

Willingness to personalize the learning experience. Instruction falls short if it does not at least provide a context, a frame of reference, or some direct way to apply what is being taught. Alerting students to obstacles they may encounter, making frequent and specific references to the assignment, and incorporating personal stories and anecdotes are good ways of doing so.

Patience. Instruction librarians may regularly need to place their own agendas on hold. What a librarian needs and wants to teach may be different from that of the person requesting the instruction. In addition, every student comes to class with a different set of skills, abilities, motivations, and expectations. Many may have good computer skills but be relatively unfamiliar with the research process, or vice versa. Instructors need to be patient and work with students at their own level and pace.

Sense of humor. Telling jokes or trying to be funny should not be confused with having a sense of humor. Having a sense of humor means being positive and optimistic, remaining upbeat, and not taking things personally. The benefits are obvious. Telling jokes or otherwise injecting humor into a class is a good way to build rapport. There is, however, a danger of seeming unprofessional or not worthy of being taken seriously. There is also the risk of upsetting or offending someone with a particular joke.

Organizational skills. It is important to come to class prepared. This means having an orderly, logical sequence to and clear expectations about whatever content is being conveyed. Offering organized, well-structured instruction keeps students focused. It also provides a means for assessment and a greater measure of accountability. Being organized, though, also means sticking to the topic or plan and limiting the infusion of personal opinions and values. This is especially true for one-shot sessions where time is limited.

Speaking skills. Even the best instruction falls short if no one can hear or understand what is being said. The value of good articulation, the use of inflection (i.e., avoid speaking in monotone), proper grammar, and an appropriate rate and level of speech should not be overlooked.

Ability to teach people, not content. Many are under the mistaken impression that teaching is simply a matter of conveying content. Effectiveness is much more than simply the degree to which all of the scheduled content is delivered. Good instructors find new, creative, and interesting ways to talk about old things. They are sensitive to their audience and attempt to engage everyone in the class in the learning process through a variety of techniques and activities.

Respect for privacy and confidentiality. This is imperative. Student grades and other performance measures, behavior in class, and discussions about controversial or "personal" issues/concerns should not be shared. Although this may seem like an obvious thing in a classroom or in the midst of a group of students, it is also inappropriate to talk about such things with colleagues at the water fountain or in the halls after a class. When such information is shared—accidentally or on purpose—it severely undermines students' and your colleagues' trust in your effectiveness as an instructor.

Value as positive role model. Be a good example and live what you teach. Effective teachers exhibit and try to foster attitudes and behaviors that promote and encourage learning. They also teach skills that promote learning within and beyond the classroom.

Ability to listen. The value of being a good listener cannot be overemphasized. This is true for your students who are comfortable talking but perhaps even more so for those who are not. Some students ask no questions because they are shy, others because they do not want to appear stupid. Still others do not speak in class but may seek out the instructor after the class has concluded. If at any time an instructor seems reluctant or unable to listen, students are likely to shut down and disengage themselves from the class.

Professionalism. Sharing personal anecdotes is a great way to build rapport and add relevance to instruction, but instructors need to know where to draw the line. For example, there is no excuse for criticizing colleagues or other instructors, bemoaning budget shortfalls, or getting on your soapbox about whatever issue concerns you that day. You are the professional and are expected to appear and otherwise act as such.

Ability to provide closure. Closure allows individuals to see the respective parts of a concept or skill as part of a larger whole. By stepping back and seeing how all of the pieces fit together, students are more likely to retain what they learn. They are also more likely to be able to transfer this knowledge to multiple contexts and tasks.

Authenticity. Be yourself and be genuine. If you lack sincerity, it is extremely difficult to get students to respect you or to value what you are presenting to them. Similarly, welcome questions. When you do not know an answer, be honest; it is okay to admit it. In such circumstances, though, always try to exchange contact information so you can follow up later.

Lack of concern for recognition. The best teachers do not teach for the recognition. In fact, the value of teaching often goes unrecognized. Those who teach need to be comfortable not receiving any direct recognition for their efforts, if they receive any recognition at all. Because the product of instruction is often abstract and intangible, instructors must simply value learning and focus on the many and varied contributions they make to the learning process—however nebulous and difficult it may be to characterize those contributions. This is particularly true in a library setting. When we teach, we often never see the impact on our students. When students learn how to search for and use information, who knows where it can lead? Graduate school, career path changes, lifestyle choices, and more are all directly affected by the instruction we provide.

Composure. Do not take things personally. Always strive to maintain your perspective. It is frustrating to teach a class when students ask no questions or do not follow up after class for in-depth assistance. Though not common, indifference, rude behavior, and even outright threats are also not uncommon. Regardless, to be effective and remain credible, instructors cannot take such behavior personally. Accept it for what it is and do not dwell on it.

NINE CHARACTERISTICS OF EFFECTIVE INSTRUCTION

EVEN THE MOST EXPERIENCED of instructors can fail to be effective if their presentations fall short. Unfortunately, there is no magical list of things that instructors can do to ensure success in all situations. Worse, some of the things that can ruin an otherwise good lesson are beyond the control of the instructor, such as when the network crashes on the day of a scheduled class, rendering access to the websites to be discussed impossible.

Still, there are elements that do contribute to effective instruction and that are under the control of the instructor. Those associated specifically with the instructor are outlined in chapter 8, and those associated with how students learn are discussed in chapter 3. This chapter focuses on some of the many specific things that make for a more effective presentation of the actual content of a lesson.

STRATEGIES

The strategies outlined in this section are generally applicable to all presentations and contexts. They are not dependent upon the instructor, method of instruction, location, or any of a number factors that tend to be more context- or presentation-specific. Rather, they are examples of some of the things that every instructor should take into account with every instruction session.

Practice. The value of practicing one's presentation beforehand cannot be over-emphasized. Being prepared is particularly important for new instructors and those who teach infrequently as well as for presentations being given in an unfamiliar location. Among other benefits, practicing enables instructors to identify and address potential problems with their content and presentation. It also lets them know if they have too much or too little content.

Have a backup plan. No matter how much they plan and practice, every instructor experiences problems at one time or another. The computers in the classroom may not be working the day of your class, or the network may be down. Because computers and networks can be unstable, having all of your notes and handouts saved to a removable storage device is always a good idea. You might also e-mail your files to yourself as a second precaution. At the very least, you should have printed copies of your lesson notes and instructional materials with you. Although this is not ideal, at least you can still proceed through your lesson when the equipment you planned to use is not working or is unavailable.

Know your audience. Talking "below" your students is as bad as talking "above" them. Instructors should always strive to match their content, word choices, and overall lesson plans to their students and their needs. That is why having a specific assignment or set of objectives to meet is so crucial. Even so, the terms and concepts you would use to speak to a group of medical students about bacteria, for example, should be dramatically different than those used with a group of fifth-grade science students.

Pace yourself. Instructors need a sense of how long they will spend on each component of a given class or lesson. Generally speaking, the more time devoted to a topic, the more significance students attach to it. Yet time must also be allotted for questions. This is a difficult balancing act, for there is no way to predict the number of questions or how long it will take to address them. Instructors need to be as prepared to fill empty space as they are to reduce time spent on or even eliminate certain topics when a class runs too long. Either way, it is important to stay within the allotted time frame whenever possible. Having a watch or clock nearby and checking it periodically throughout your presentation help in this regard.

Wear comfortable clothing you feel good in. Aside from adding to your comfort, this is a simple yet subtle way to increase your confidence. Remember, though, that your appearance should always be professional, tasteful, and appropriate to the audience. If you are teaching in an unfamiliar location, you should consider dressing in layers in case the room is too hot or too cold.

Follow up. Many instructors overlook the fact that a class does not end when the lesson is over. Students often have questions or need additional, in-depth assistance. Instructors need to make themselves available, either immediately after class or via individually scheduled appointments. Sharing your contact information and times of availability (e.g. office hours, reference desk) is strongly recommended. It is also good to follow up with the classroom instructor. Among other things, this helps you determine the degree to which the class objectives have been met, what could have been covered more or less, and if additional classes need to be scheduled.

Manage your body language. One's body language can have a dramatic impact on the effectiveness of instruction. Looking interested and maintaining eye contact are certainly critical. But there are also subtle things an instructor can do to enhance instruction. Among others are using your hands to add emphasis and varying not only where you look but for how often and for how long. Rather than stand behind the desk or podium, another simple thing you can do is move around the room. This not only adds visual interest for the students, it also makes you seem more approachable and involved.

Decide when to distribute handouts. Deciding when to distribute handouts might seem like a simple question. Instructors need to be aware, though, that the timing of such can have an impact on the general flow of instruction. Distributed at the start, for example, handouts are helpful for students to use as guides and can be used to take notes. However, they may also be a distraction and draw away from the presentation. Distributed at the end, handouts serve as an ideal supplement to or reminder about the presentation. But doing so risks students not being able to remember or even know how the content on the handout relates to the material presented in class or how to apply such in a meaningful way.

TACTICS

In contrast to the strategies outlined above, tactics are specific things one can do to enhance the impact of presentations. There are countless books, articles, websites, and other resources that deal with these issues, and I do not attempt to list them all. What follows is merely a cross section of some typical categories and a few common suggestions associated with each.

Spoken/Auditory Elements

- Maintain a constant yet appropriate speed.
- Use tone and inflection to generate interest, add emphasis, and maintain attention.
- Talk to the back of the room to help ensure that everyone can hear you.
- Ask the students to get involved by asking questions and requesting opinions.
- Talk—do not read or simply regurgitate memorized notes.

Visual Elements

- Plan content knowing that eyes tend to focus on the middle of visual presentations.
- Balance your content and leave plenty of space to avoid crowding.
- Make sure your content is obvious and text is clear.
- Triple-check to be sure your text is free of typographical errors and misspellings.
- Give clear and proper credit for content that is not your own.

Using Visual Aids and Images/Video

- Be sure images are clear and can be seen and read by the audience.
- Be sure images contribute content (not just add visual appeal) or help to clarify a particular point or concept.
- Do not overuse images or videos—less is usually more.
- Avoid lengthy video clips and overly complex charts, tables, and other images.

Multimedia: Presentation

- Remember that the presentation is only an aid to the instruction, not the instruction itself.
- If possible before the session, try your presentation in the location where you will be presenting.
- Distribute paper copies or make electronic copies of your presentation available.
- Use pointers sparingly and avoid "laser light shows" at all costs.

Multimedia: Formatting

- Use large, simple fonts. 18–50 point size is often recommended.
- When preparing slides, use a template to help ensure consistent fonts, colors, and other formatting.
- Use a background that contrasts with your text. A dark background with light text tends to work best.
- Limit the total number of slides.
- Keep slides focused. Seven words per line, seven lines per slide, and one to two minutes per slide.

A Note on the Use of Clip Art

There are mixed opinions about the use of clip art, whether as part of a handout or a multimedia presentation. On the plus side, clip art is readily available, often directly via the software application being used. This accessibility makes clip art convenient. Even when it is not part of the software, finding and incorporating clip art into a project is fairly straightforward and typically requires minimal effort and cost. It is also a great way to break up the monotony of text-only pages and screens.

Unfortunately, clip art also has its downsides. First and foremost, the value of white space should not be underestimated. Too many images—of any kind—can be as bad as (or worse than) no images at all. They can be distracting and significantly distract the viewer's attention from the main points being expressed. The generic look of clip art in particular can make a presentation appear unprofessional, especially if used frequently. Its widespread availability can also suggest indifference or laziness on the part of the instructor.

When developing courses and other curricular materials, instructors need to closely examine the images they are using. The tactics listed above for visual and multimedia presentations can also be applied to clip art. But, whether it is a clip art image, a sketch, a photograph, or some other imagery, instructors should always strive to find the most appropriate, not necessarily the most readily available, image to place into their work.

MANAGING THINGS THAT CAN DISRUPT A LESSON

No matter how much time is spent developing a class or lecture, there are still any number of things that can derail even the best-prepared instructors. As noted above, instructors need to be prepared for inevitable technological problems. But the things that can derail a class are not always technology-related. Being aware of these problems can go a long way toward successfully navigating them if and when they arise in class.

Answering Questions during a Presentation

You cannot anticipate how many questions you will receive in a class or how long it will take to address them. If instructors budget too much time for questions, they are faced with the real possibility of running out of lesson material before the class ends. On the other hand, if they budget insufficient time, they risk not being able to cover everything in their lesson plan or having the class run over its allotted time.

The bottom line is that you should never fail to try to answer a student's question. If you do not answer, you risk having students focus on the unanswered question. And do not ask students to hold their questions until the end of class. This could be interpreted to mean that you do not know how to respond or are uncomfortable answering.

Suggestions

- Repeat the question so that everyone hears it.
- Maintain eye contact with the person who posed the question.
- Do not try to bluff if someone asks you a question you cannot answer. Admit that you do not know or cannot recall the answer.
- If you offer to answer the question or provide assistance after class, be sure you follow through. Do not make promises you do not intend to keep.
- If someone asks a question about something you will address later in the course, give a brief answer and say you will provide a fuller response later.

Avoiding Bodily Embarrassments

There is no polite way of discussing this topic. Suffice it to say that sometimes our bodies are not our best friends. Excessive yawning, stomach grumblings, and worse are distracting and can be more than a little embarrassing. They can also be extremely disruptive to a class and should be reduced or eliminated whenever possible.

Suggestions

- Use perfumes or colognes sparingly for they may cause allergic reactions or at least discomfort among students, particularly in one-on-one instruction.
- Avoid foods prior to class that you know cause you to become thirsty, produce phlegm, or generate unpleasant odors.
- Get a good night's sleep prior to days on which you will be teaching.
- Avoid chewing gum; it can interfere with your speech and detract from your credibility.
- Avoid caffeinated or sugared beverages. If you are going to keep any sort of beverage nearby, water is always recommended. In any case, keep your drink in a sealed container and in a place where you are unlikely to spill it.

Combating Nerves

Not everyone is comfortable speaking in front of a group. Even the most experienced instructors sometimes experience varying degrees of stage fright. Just remember, you are the professional, the one they are coming to see. There are really only two reasons you should ever be nervous: when you are worried about what others will think of you, and when you are unprepared.

Suggestions

- Always be prepared and focus on what you are there to do for your audience.
- Avoid "nervous speak." Consider placing reminders like *pause* or *breathe* in your lesson notes.
- Do not take things personally.

Dealing with Absent Instructors or Instructors Who Leave during Class

Instruction librarians need to decide how long they are prepared to wait for the attending teacher to arrive. They also need to have a plan of action if the attending teacher does not show up at all. The importance of your class is significantly diminished when the attending teacher does not attend the class or leaves before it is over. Among other things, this suggests to the students that the teacher does not value the lesson—so why should they? It also puts the librarian in the awkward position of having to answer questions about the assignment—questions he may not be able to answer, further compromising his credibility.

Rest assured, most teachers would never think of behaving this unprofessionally. Most who request instruction value its importance and attend without incident. Those who fail to, though, typically have perfectly legitimate reasons (e.g., illness, car accident). Still, there are a few who view library instruction as a way to free up their schedules; they schedule library instruction because they want to use the time to do something else. Worse, sometimes the instruction librarian is not forewarned that the attending instructor will not be attending.

Suggestions

- If the teacher do not show up, do not cancel the class out of spite. In the end, it is your class and you have to decide if it is more beneficial to hold the class without the teacher than to not hold the class at all. After all, you already have a lesson you are prepared to administer.
- Use the first absence or departure as a chance for dialogue. The teacher may simply feel no need to be in class or may not understand the mixed message her absence sends to students. Hold the class and, afterward, contact the teacher, politely informing her of the reasons her attendance is expected in the future. Possible talking points include sharing questions you received but could not answer; discussing discipline problems you encountered; noting how waiting forced you to reduce or eliminate activities or discussion of certain concepts and content; and sharing how students reacted to her absence.

Managing Disruptive Behavior

What constitutes "disruptive" is relative. Everyone has different levels of patience and tolerance for handling disruptive behavior. What is too loud for one may be perfectly acceptable to another. Because library or the instructing librarian's policies may be different from classroom or the regular instructor's policies, students need to be made aware what the rules are at the start of a class. Even if there are no explicit rules, instruction librarians need a sense of what they will do if such behavior emerges.

At the same time, instructors need to be cautioned about being overbearing. Things are not always clear-cut. Disruptive activities need to be placed in context, and instructors need to exercise judgment. Kicking a student out of class because a cell phone rings is not necessarily the right response. Although it is likely that the student simply forgot to shut off a phone, it is just as likely that there is a legitimate emergency. Either way, informing students at the start of class about your cell phone policy can help to eliminate any awkward confrontation during class. Students will then know what the consequences are likely to be should a cell phone ring. Likewise, this gives a chance for someone to alert you beforehand that they might be receiving a call they need to answer.

Suggestions

- If you or the library have specific behavioral expectations (e.g., no cell phones), share them as well as the consequences of those expectations not being met at the start of class.
- Remember that not all talking is bad. Learn to distinguish meaningful from disruptive talking. A student should not be penalized, for example, for asking a neighbor to repeat what was just said. In contrast, disruptive talking intrudes upon the conducive, nurturing learning environment you are trying to create and is typically characterized by speech that is loud, irrelevant to the nature of the class, and ongoing.

- Do not become confrontational. Attacking the disruptive student tends to make you look bad and often results in students sympathizing with the person causing the disruption.
- Disruptive behavior is often a cry for attention. You should avoid confronting students, because it only adds to the drama they are hoping to create in the first place by drawing attention to themselves.
- Diffuse a disruptive student politely. Ask if he has a question or if something is unclear. If not and the student continues talking, it is not inappropriate to ask him to leave. This will cause a temporary stir among students, but one that tends to dissipate pretty rapidly and is generally far less disruptive than allowing the talking to continue.

Dealing with Emergencies

Though emergencies are rare, instruction librarians need to be prepared to deal with them. Sometimes they are organized and librarians are aware of them ahead of time, as in the case of a planned fire drill or power outage. But true emergencies arise with little to no warning. Examples include anything from a student passing out in class to a student exhibiting threatening behavior or a computer suddenly exploding into flames. In these situations, do your best to remain calm and to keep everyone safe until professional help arrives.

Suggestions

- Become familiar with your institution's safety and emergency procedures, and do your best to follow them in a crisis.
- Make a mental note of the location of fire extinguishers and emergency exits for the room in which you are teaching.
- If a student threatens you outright or acts in a manner that makes you feel uncomfortable, do not hesitate to contact the police or security staff. At the very least, ask the attending instructor or a student to remain with you after class until you can get someplace you feel safe.

TEN ASSESSMENT

AN ASSESSMENT, SOMETIMES REFERRED to as an *evaluation* or *review*, can be a one-time activity or an ongoing process. However it is construed, at a fundamental level an assessment involves both the identification of a need and the collection of data to better understand the need. Though the specific reasons for conducting assessments vary, data collected from assessments of instruction are typically used to suggest changes at the instructor, course, or programmatic level. Such data can be generated through informal means such as feedback or more formal measures such as surveys and tests.

Because of variations in both instructional techniques and instructional objectives, there is no single method of assessment or means of collecting data that can be used in all settings, by all individuals, or at all libraries. Although having some knowledge of assessment concepts and procedures is helpful, it is beyond the scope of this book to both detail and describe how to conduct an actual assessment. Still, although the specifics vary, all forms of assessment share some features, issues, and challenges.

INFORMAL ASSESSMENT

In instances where no formal assessment occurs, instruction librarians should always make some sort of an effort to both give and receive informal feedback after a class has concluded. Because this sort of information is typically collected on a case-by-case basis rather than systematically, it often lacks consistency. Still, even though not an assessment in the strictest sense of the word, an informal follow-up with students and the attending faculty member after a class can generate extremely useful information, especially for modifying existing lessons or developing new content and classes.

Informal feedback also supplies insights into topics and issues that more formal assessments typically do not address. Some teachers and students may not feel comfortable sharing certain information during class, or there may simply not be a way to do this on a formal assessment. Such individuals may feel more comfortable sharing such information during a more personal, one-on-one follow-up session after class.

In general, it is important always to keep in mind that teaching does not end when the lesson is over. Students often have questions, perhaps something they did not get to ask in class. Or you may want to confer with the classroom instructor to determine what worked and what was ineffective. Many instructors underestimate the amount of time following up with students and teachers after a class can take. In fact, it can often take as much time as the actual lesson itself, if not more.

Following Up with the Classroom Teacher

After the class is over, discussing the class with the classroom teacher is important. This provides an opportunity for both individuals to identify problems and issues that detracted from the class as well as strengths that made it successful. In turn, this information can be used to effect better assignments and improve the lesson.

Discussion Suggestions

- Focus on your instruction and pedagogy, not the classroom teacher's.
- Investigate changes that could improve the effectiveness of the lesson or assignment.
- Identify objectives that were met and not met and the reasons for these results.
- Discuss difficulties experienced before, during, and after the class, such as discipline, technology, or presentation.
- Schedule additional sessions as needed.

Cautions

- Be prepared to be criticized.
- The instructor may be defensive, particularly when discussing assignments.
- Not every instructor will be open to meeting with you.
- Have an agenda or specific set of questions and discussion points.
- Keep conversation professional, not personal.

Following Up with Students

During a class, it is imperative that you always share your contact information as well as preferred dates and times for scheduling small-group or one-on-one follow-up sessions. Likewise, let students know your preferred format of contact (e.g., e-mail, phone) and when they can reasonably expect a response.

There are two ways of establishing follow-up with students: student-initiated requests and librarian-initiated requests. Both provide a great opportunity to build rapport, enhance your credibility as a librarian, and ultimately generate positive feelings toward the library. But follow-up can also have a dark side if it is not conducted properly and in a timely manner.

Librarian-Initiated Follow-Up

Some instructors contact students directly after a class, but to reduce any appearance of impropriety instructors should refrain from requesting a student's personal contact information unless there is a specific context for doing so. For example, after having worked with the student in class, the instructor may have additional information or insight to share about the student's project or have an answer to a question he was unable to answer for the student in class. In this case, it is not inappropriate to ask for contact information or to speak with the student the next time you encounter him.

Unsolicited contact, though, is inappropriate. If a student does not know why she is being contacted, at the very least you risk being accused of stereotyping (e.g., racism, sexism, ageism). If you do decide to contact a student and the student does not respond to your initial follow-up, repeated attempts to contact her could result in claims of harassment or worse. Even mere rumors of impropriety are difficult to contain and—real or imagined—can severely compromise your credibility as an instructor. Depending on the severity and legitimacy of the claim, such rumors can quickly put your career in jeopardy, with the distinct possibility of causing significant collateral damage to your personal life as well.

Student-Initiated Follow-Up

The more common scenario is for a student or group of students to contact an instructor after class to schedule an appointment or request additional help or information. This should not be seen as evidence that you are an ineffective teacher. Particularly for students with little library or research experience, the information presented in class may simply be too overwhelming or too much to remember. Others may be reluctant to ask questions in front of their peers or may not have been able to have their specific need or question addressed before class was over.

That said, in this age of litigation and liability it is not a bad idea to have a colleague sit in whenever there is even a hint that a problem is brewing. Dissatisfaction with a grade or when a disruptive student is involved are but two examples. In a worst-case scenario (when a student has threatened you with harm), you need to decide if you are the right person to be talking with the student. If you think you are, having someone else present provides an added layer of physical safety. It also ensures that a witness is present to whatever is said or done.

FORMAL ASSESSMENT

Although informal feedback can be a great source of information, it has its drawbacks. First of all, not everyone participates in the process. So, necessarily, the data will be skewed. It is also not systematic. Everyone is different, and therefore every feedback experience is likely to be different as well. As a result, developing meaningful comparisons and drawing accurate conclusions are very difficult, if not impossible.

For these and other reasons, more formal assessments are also used to provide data about instruction librarians and library instruction classes and programs. Such assessments can vary considerably from library to library. Still, they tend to be similar in terms of the steps involved with the process. There are essentially eight steps or stages shared by every assessment:

1. Identify why you are doing an assessment.

2. Decide what is to be assessed.

3. Determine what data to collect.

4. Identify an appropriate tool to collect the data.

5. Administer the tool.

6. Analyze the data.

7. Interpret the data.

8. Apply the results.

Step 1: Identify Why You Are Doing an Assessment

Simply put, we live in an age of accountability. As in other facets of society, budget limitations, personnel cutbacks, changing demographics, information technology, and a host of other factors are placing libraries and librarians under increased scrutiny. To that end, administrators as well as those who utilize library resources and services are increasingly examining whether or not we are doing what we say we are doing. A central part of this endeavor is determining the degree to which we are effective at meeting their needs and expectations. This can be especially true for those who provide instruction because of the direct, visible contact we have with students and the curricular process. Instruction librarians who are successful in meeting their objectives are more likely to receive funding, to be allowed to generate additional programming, and so on. Those who are not are more likely to be marginalized or have their services overhauled or even canceled entirely.

Five broad, common purposes for conducting assessments are outlined below. To enable meaningful comparisons among the data, good assessments typically fall within a single category. Hybrid approaches—those incorporating elements from more than one category—are not uncommon and are not necessarily invalid, but they run the risk of generating a lot of general, surface-level sorts of information. The converse can also be true: they generate so much detail that interpreting the results in a meaningful way can be a challenge.

Organizational. Because they occur at the institutional or organizational level, assessments in this context are typically broader in scope. The assessment might be a single, one-time requirement, such as when the library is asked to supply assessment data as part of an accreditation process. At other times, though, these assessments are library-specific, such as when a library conducts its annual periodic review or updates its strategic plan.

Professional. Librarians are often asked to supply assessment data for various professional reasons such as evaluation portfolios, sabbatical proposals, and promotion applications. The data may be about the instructor, the instruction, or both. Often the data are standardized to enable comparisons between individuals performing similar tasks.

Pedagogical. This type of assessment is used primarily to determine if the instruction met the desired objectives—if students learned what they were expected to learn or acquired the skills they were expected to acquire as a result of the instruction. In some cases, one form or aspect of instruction may be compared to another in an attempt to determine which is more effective (e.g., hands-on vs. lecture).

Presentational. These assessments revolve around gathering data as a means of identifying strengths and weaknesses of an instructor's style or presentation. Among other things, the instructor's clarity of speech, openness to questions, and speed of delivery might be rated by students. Likewise, if an instructor uses some form of multimedia (e.g., PowerPoint slide show), students might evaluate things such as the effectiveness of the presentation's color scheme or readability of the fonts used.

Administrative. This form of assessment is not nearly as common as those described above. As the name suggests, administrative assessment looks at things associated with the administration of the instruction itself. Among other things, this might include such things as costs (e.g., photocopying, compensation), time (e.g., preparation, in-class, follow-up), and resources needed or used (e.g., physical space, seating).

Suggestions

- Do not conduct an assessment unless you have a clear purpose in mind.
- Be sure the reason for conducting the assessment is clearly articulated to *everyone* involved.
- Decide if an assessment can be modified to meet multiple purposes.
- Focus. Do not try to do too much with a single assessment.

Step 2: Decide What Is to Be Assessed

At some level and to varying degrees, it can be argued that all assessments are ultimately designed to provide information about something, alter practice, change policy, or some combination thereof. Even so, one of the key challenges to assessment is deciding what is to be assessed. Variations in teaching styles and content are just two of the factors that can quickly confound this process. For example, because of different needs, content, and other factors, there is often considerable variation between classes. This makes it difficult to develop a consistent, meaningful assessment that works with all classes. These sorts of issues become even more problematic when more than one person is providing instruction, since specific resources used, features taught, and teaching methods used are likely to vary even more.

In the end, the short answer to what to assess is twofold. First, whatever is to be assessed needs to be measurable. If something cannot be measured or the data collected are not meaningful, the value of the assessment is severely compromised. Second, what is assessed should always be aligned with the reasons the class is being taught in the first place; instruction provided should always be evaluated primarily in terms of meeting the established objectives or standards for the class. If a workshop is developed to help students find books in the library, an assessment of students' ability to use an index to locate articles is inappropriate. Though it might provide valuable information, such an assessment would be beyond the scope of this particular workshop objective.

Aligning instruction with some sort of course objectives generally takes place in one of two ways. Those providing instruction often develop their own objectives, criteria, and evaluative tools and conduct assessments accordingly based on a perceived need or context. In some cases, these objectives are developed in conjunction with another librarian or teacher; in others, they are developed independently. Either way, the value of such assessments is often double-edged. They are still common and do have value, particularly in helping address specific issues and concerns. At the same time, they risk being too specific or subjective to be of much use to anyone or to any setting other than the one in which the assessment took place.

For these and other reasons, an increasing number of courses and instruction programs are incorporating some form of clearly articulated, established, or otherwise recognized objectives. These might also be referred to by such terms as *standards, learning outcomes,* or *performance indicators.* Such standards can be developed locally, such as those designed to meet specific assignment-related goals and objectives. They may also be more broad-based, as in the Information Literacy Competency Standards for Higher Education developed by ACRL. At whatever level and however they come about, clear objectives provide a consistent or standard means by which instruction can be assessed.

With the above in mind, there are essentially four types of standards or objectives upon which assessment of library instruction is generally built:

External. Sometimes the standards used to assess library instruction have been developed or established outside of the library. Such standards tend to be general in scope and have broad application. School districts, for example, have standards by which all teachers and instruction within the district are assessed. A growing number of professional library organizations and accrediting bodies provide standards and expectations for library instruction. Even public libraries often have to deal with some form of community standards. In cases where such standards are not geared specifically to library instruction, they can often be adapted relatively easily.

Curricular. This type of objective revolves around the curriculum and the students themselves. There may be specific student learning objectives and outcomes identified by the school, by the institution, or by a given department. There may also be expectations or outcomes specified in a course outline, syllabus, or individual assignment. Curricular objectives tend to be precise, practical sorts of things such as learning how to find articles on a particular topic or learning how a classification scheme is used to shelve books.

Library. In addition to the professional standards noted above, individual libraries may also have specific goals, objectives, and learning outcomes for their instruction programs, classes, or instruction librarians. These may be geared specifically to instruction or can be part of a larger assessment of the library as a whole.

Personal. Librarians may have additional objectives they set for themselves. Typically these are used for personal or professional development purposes (e.g., personnel files) or to make their instruction more relevant, engaging, or beneficial to the participants. For example, to improve his presentation, a librarian may wish to assess whether students think she talks too fast or too slow as a means of determining if she should alter her speed of delivery.

Suggestions

- Decide if a single assessment is sufficient or if multiple assessments are more appropriate.
- Ensure that objectives align from top to bottom as well as from bottom to top.
- Determine the level of and degree to which any one issue, objective, or topic is to be assessed.
- Do not administer a previous assessment without examining it for relevance and appropriateness in the current context.
- Articulate what is to be considered "success," "effective," or "proficient."

Step 3: Determine What Data to Collect

After deciding what is to be assessed, your next step is determining what types of data need to be collected. To this end, there are three types of data typically collected during an assessment: participant, class, and assessment data.

Participant Data

Participant data inform the researcher of the characteristics of the sample population being studied, the students in the class. Such data enable those conducting the assessment to develop a meaningful context for the data collected. This information also alerts the instructor to trends and patterns that can then be used to make informed decisions about developing and administering action plans to address needs and shortcomings. Though by no means exhaustive, categories of commonly requested participant data are gender, age (or student level, e.g., freshman, junior, graduate), grade point average, degree program, and familiarity with the library and its resources (e.g., typical number of uses per week, self-report of comfort using resources, number of term papers written).

Class Data

Whereas participant data are reflective of the individuals in the class, class data are more general and refer to characteristics of the class. Collecting class data is optional and is typically associated with an internal, local need or usage (e.g., program review, annual report). On a practical level, it is particularly useful for scheduling purposes.

Common types of class data recorded for classes are number of students in the class, class name or section, topics covered, time/day/week class is held, and name of classroom instructor.

Suggestions

- Determine if the desired data already exist.
- Do not collect superfluous, irrelevant, or inappropriate data.
- Identify specific, measurable elements of a class, assignment, or objective to be measured and collect data accordingly.
- If possible, determine alternate ways of collecting similar data on the same topic to provide a variety of different perspectives.

Assessment Data

Assessment data address the specific questions or concerns of the assessment. These are the data collected on the situation or problem being studied. Which data are collected depends on the purpose of the evaluation. For example, the data needed to determine whether students have *actually* learned how to perform a particular task are different from the data collected to determine if they *believe* they have learned to perform the task. With that in mind, the following represent two of the key data elements to consider when determining the type of data to collect as part of an assessment. Some assessments may focus on only one element; others may incorporate some of each. Instruction librarians need to find the appropriate balance.

Static vs. dynamic data. Static data reflect students' knowledge of the concepts and ideas presented in class. These data are typically collected for classes that focus on developing awareness of library terms, concepts, and resources. For example, a class might teach students the name of and access points to the library's catalog without teaching students how to actually use the catalog. For this reason, assessments producing static data are typically associated with things like tours and general library orientations.

Dynamic, or performance, data demonstrate students' ability to perform a particular task or otherwise show how well they have acquired the desired skill. Using the above example, a student might be asked to access the library's catalog and identify the call number and location of a particular book. This type of data is particularly useful when assessing student learning outcomes that emphasize practical, applied sorts of knowledge rather than conceptual, philosophical types.

Subjective vs. objective data. Subjective data are responses generated by the subjects themselves and are typically associated with short-answer and essay questions. The big advantage of subjective questions is that individuals can detail what they mean and discuss issues not present or addressed by the evaluation. However, because they are unique, subjective data make meaningful comparisons among individuals difficult and, in some cases, impossible.

Objective data are couched in consistent terms and enable comparisons among individuals. Questions where individuals are asked to indicate yes or no or to rank an item on a scale are good examples. The answers are consistent. Despite this consistency, it is not always clear what such data mean or imply. For example, one person might indicate "good" and another person "very good," even though they feel exactly the same way about the thing they are evaluating.

Step 4: Identify an Appropriate Tool to Collect the Data

Determining which tool or instrument to use to collect data goes hand in hand with deciding which type of data to collect; the instrument selected should be appropriate to the type of information to be collected. Surveys, for example, are useful for collecting opinions and attitudes about something, whereas tests are good for measuring skill attainment or content mastery. There are a variety of tools and methods used to collect data. These tools can be developed internally, externally, or as a combination of the two.

Internally Developed

Internally developed assessments tend to be specific to an individual instructor, library, or class. Their main value lies in their capacity to focus on the problems, activities, and other issues and concerns unique to a given course, assignment, or instructor. For example, an instructor may wish to collect data about relative strengths and weaknesses of his presentation style. Because the instructor is generally very familiar with the matter to be assessed, development of appropriate questions and activities is fairly straightforward and focused for him.

Such assessments are not without problems. First and foremost, even though the librarian may be well aware of the issues and the questions she wants to ask, generating a suitable instrument to assess them can be extremely time consuming. The time spent on developing appropriate wordings of questions, deciding what type of response option to use (e.g., ranking, multiple choice), and piloting the instrument should not be underestimated.

Establishing validity can be even more difficult. On the one hand, the specificity and subjective nature of internally developed tools often generate results that have little or no meaning or value outside of the context in which they were developed and administered. On the other hand, without sufficient piloting and modification, internally developed assessments may lead respondents—purposely or accidentally— toward a particular answer. For example, the instructor may only ask questions he knows will place him in a favorable light or will lead students to the answer he would like them to supply.

Externally Developed

Externally developed assessments tend to be more structured and are often standardized. By definition, they are developed by an individual, group, or organization outside of the library. Their more objective nature virtually eliminates personality from the assessment process and makes it possible to draw similar comparisons across multiple classes or instructors. Externally developed assessments may be available for free, but often they have some sort of cost associated with their acquisition or administration.

Because they have often been tested for things such as reliability and validity, externally developed assessments tend to provide more universalizable data. This makes them particularly useful for providing program-level data and for examining broad, general sorts of issues. Still, this one-size-fits-all approach can pose problems. Among others, being standardized does not inherently mean being objective. In addition, it does not necessarily allow for individual variations between instructors, students, or courses. It also risks missing the forest for the trees in that little things can get glossed over, if they are even noticed at all.

Shared Models

Shared or hybrid assessments combine both internally and externally developed elements and can reflect the best of both. Sometimes only certain aspects of an externally developed assessment, for example, are relevant locally. At the same time, they may lack the desired degree or amount of specificity. Elements may need to be adapted or otherwise incorporated into the external assessment to better align with local issues and concerns.

Suggestions

- Identify the costs, training, licensing, and similar concerns associated with use of the instrument.
- Allow enough time to pilot a self-developed instrument adequately before administering it.
- When self-developing an instrument, contact individuals, examine books, and consult other resources to determine the best approach.
- Determine what, if any, restrictions (e.g., copyright) apply to using content from others' instruments.

Step 5: Administer the Tool

Having developed an instrument, the next step is to actually administer it. Again, this may sound easier than it is. Both broad ethical and practical considerations become relevant to the assessment.

Suggestions

- Inform participants of how the data will be used.
- Maintain participants' anonymity and confidentiality.
- Allow enough time to complete the assessment.
- Provide adequate and appropriate instructions.
- Articulate participants' role as responders or context for responses (e.g., respond to specific assignment/course or as students in general).

There are specific issues that need to be considered as well. A few of these are reviewed below.

Choosing the Type of Participation

Participation in an assessment can be required or voluntary. Requiring participation obviously guarantees a greater rate of return, but coordinating the assessment can be a challenge. If you conduct it during class, the amount of time available for instruction diminishes accordingly. If you conduct it outside of class, you must work with the attending faculty member to determine how to ensure that everyone participates.

When participation is voluntary, the rate of return is typically much lower, since only those who want to respond or perceive value in doing so respond. Not using valuable class time or having to coordinate the assessment with the attending instructor are key advantages. The big risk, though, is that the data may be skewed because you hear only from some class members.

Offering Participation Incentives

Sometimes instructors incorporate some sort of incentive (e.g., extra credit, cash) for participating in an assessment. The intent is to generate greater rates of participation. However, incentives can backfire, and instructors need to be cautious. For example, depending on how they are characterized, incentives risk being perceived as bribes. Even if they are not, they risk generating "please me, please you" responses; because they are being rewarded, participants may respond more favorably or in the way they feel the assessor wants them to respond.

Equally problematic is that an incentive may actually function as a sort of disincentive. If the assessment is offered only as extra credit (i.e., it is not required), weak and strong students alike may perceive it as little more than busywork and not respond. In addition, students may not feel it is worth their effort to complete the assessment for extra credit. In such cases, again, the data are biased toward those who complete the assessment and are not necessarily representative of the sample population (the whole class).

Choosing a Delivery Method

Pen-and-paper assessments are still common. They are often machine-readable, reducing the amount of time spent compiling the data. They do, however, require time to distribute and collect. They are also prone to legibility problems; students may not completely erase an answer before changing it, or they may misalign their answers to the questions, especially with longer or more involved assessments.

A growing number of assessments are being conducted electronically via the Web or local intranets. The functionality and design of these assessments are dependent upon the software and sites used. On the plus side, such assessments are easily distributed and returned, and problems with marking them are eliminated. Additionally, the results are typically compiled automatically. The technology, though, may not be available when the student is trying to access the actual assessment. It is also difficult to verify that the person completing the assessment is actually the person supposed to be doing so. In addition, the software used may not allow an individual to design the assessment exactly as desired or be flexible in terms of response options. For example, the software-imposed space or character limit for short-answer questions may be insufficient for students to respond to the desired degree.

Suggestions

- Make certain that instructions are clear and easy to follow, particularly if the assessment is not administered in person.
- Inform respondents as to how they are to respond (e.g., as themselves, a member of the class, or a person at large).
- Work with the attending instructor to coordinate the best time and type of administration.
- Determine how much time is needed to administer the tool.
- Contact others who have conducted assessments in the past for suggestions.

Step 6: Analyze the Data

Once all of the data have been collected, they need to be analyzed. Care should be taken not to equate analysis with interpretation (see step 7). *Analysis* essentially means tabulating the collected data and looking for patterns and trends. *Interpretation* means attaching meaning to the trends and patterns discovered through analysis.

Objective vs. Subjective Data Analysis

Broadly speaking, data can be analyzed in one of two ways—objectively and subjectively. Objective analysis utilizes statistical and other mathematical procedures; the interpretations are not based on personal feelings or insights. For this reason, objective analysis is associated with data measures for which the response options are the same for everyone. The use of statistics to analyze data can add a deeper layer of credibility to the results of an assessment, but lack of knowledge of or comfort level with statistics are significant obstacles for many librarians.

Subjective analysis is typically associated with data measures for which the response options are open. Common examples include short-answer and essay types of questions where respondents are asked to self-report their thoughts and feelings on a particular topic or issue. Because the data are different for each individual, the evaluator must decide what constitutes a pattern. For example, one student might respond with "OPAC" and another student with "catalog"; the person analyzing the data would need to decide if the two answers are the same or different.

Dealing with Nonresponses

No matter how data are collected, there are always some in the sample population who do not respond to some questions, whose responses are unclear, or who do not respond at all. The reasons vary: some have no interest in the topic; some feel their answers will not be kept confidential and are afraid of who might associate their answers with them; some do not know how to interpret a question or think there is no appropriate response option.

Whatever the reason for nonresponses, those conducting assessments need to have a plan in place for dealing with them *before* the assessment is administered. It is a mistake to address nonresponses after the assessment. Doing so risks jeopardizing the credibility of your data in that people could assume you are eliminating responses that you dislike or that demonstrate something contrary to what you want them to demonstrate.

Suggestions

- Do not presuppose that there is a pattern in the data.
- Double-check for data entry, transcription, and calculation errors.
- Suggest possible reasons for nonresponses.
- Do not force the analysis just to get a pattern you want.
- Consult with someone familiar with statistics and data analysis.

Step 7: Interpret the Data

Data interpretation goes hand in hand with data analysis. But whereas analysis is static, interpretation is dynamic. When interpreting the data, the evaluator attempts to assign meanings to the data trends and patterns identified through data analysis. There is no single method for interpreting data. Sometimes data patterns must be interpreted locally. Other data are consistent with trends and patterns identified in the literatures of library science, information science, and related disciplines.

Statistical vs. Practical Significance

Whether you understand statistics or not, it is important to be aware of the distinction between *statistical significance* and *practical significance*. Statistical significance is a calculated number. When something is found to be statistically significant, it simply means that the results were likely *not* caused by chance. In other words, there is likely to be some sort of significant relationship between the question and the responses. Statistical significance does not address the importance of the result—it does not imply that there is any practical significance, but it leaves open that possibility.

Conversely, practical significance *is* related to the importance of the result. Something determined to have practical significance is seen as being useful in a real-world situation or context. This, of course, is the kind of significance that is important to us as teachers.

Unexpected Patterns and Trends

By definition, expected results are expected. But unexpected patterns often appear in the data as well. Some of these can be attributed to poorly worded questions or inappropriate response options. There might also be errors in recording the data or in the mathematical operations performed on the data. But sometimes the reasons for an anomaly are not so readily discerned. In either case, it is a huge mistake to ignore these unanticipated results, particularly if they have both statistical and practical significance. Such results often provide unique insight into a problem or data about the problem from a different perspective. Ignoring them could compromise the integrity of the assessment as well as the credibility of the instructor or the instruction.

Suggestions

- Develop a working vocabulary of basic statistical terms and concepts.
- Base interpretations on the purpose of the assessment.
- Beware of imposing personal bias or agendas on the data or data patterns.
- Do not discount or discard interpretations that are uncomfortable or may be unpopular.

Step 8: Apply the Results

Applying the results can be both the most rewarding and the most frustrating part of the entire assessment process. It can be the most rewarding because this is what the assessment process is all about. Data are finally available upon which decisions can be made. But it can be frustrating when the data yield unexpected results or are inconclusive. Worse, it can also be somewhat demoralizing, for example, when a librarian thinks that she is providing good, effective instruction but the data reveal a different story.

Ultimately, collecting all the data in the world will not mean a thing if the information is not put to use somehow. Not doing something with your results seriously compromises your credibility. If individuals undergo an assessment and know the data have never been or never will be used, they will probably be less likely to take seriously or consent to an assessment in the future.

At the very least, reflect back on the original purpose of the assessment and proceed accordingly to implement some sort of recommendations based on the data. The data may suggest a change of some sort as a means of addressing a known challenge or obstacle. Or they may suggest that no changes be made, such as when something is already being done well. When the data are inconclusive or unclear, the recommendation may simply be that further investigation is warranted. Regardless of how they are used, assessment results needs to be manifested in some form of practical, meaningful outcome in order to bring suitable closure to the assessment process.

Suggestions

- Base any and all recommendations on the data.
- Record problems, issues, and concerns with conducting the assessment and work to address them the next time.

REPORTING RESULTS

Because assessment data are often reviewed by someone other than those who conduct the assessment, reporting one's findings is not always as simple as merely typing up a report with a bunch of numbers and text. Instruction librarians need to reflect on who is likely to view the results and how they will be used. Only then can they determine the best way to present the assessment findings. Addressing several key questions should help:

Depth: How much data, analysis, and interpretation are needed versus how much desired?
More numbers do not mean better results. Similarly, overinterpreting can be as bad as misinterpreting the results.

Format: How will the results be used?
Depending on the answer, a determination must be made about presentation method and medium (e.g., memo, spreadsheet, physical presentation).

Statistics: In what way and to what degree should statistics be incorporated?
Too much "statistic-ese" can quickly overwhelm an audience, but not enough may compromise the assessment's overall impact or credibility.

Audience: Where will the results be presented?
Writing for a professional journal, for example, is a lot different from presenting findings at a staff meeting.

Level: Who will be reading the results?
If nonlibrarians, library jargon and technical terms should be kept to a minimum. Terms and concepts likely to be unfamiliar should be clearly defined.

Balance: Are good, bad, and anomalous results being presented evenly and fairly?
Reports that focus on only the good or only the bad are often viewed dubiously.

ASK, "SHOULD WE BE DOING THIS?"

Few people question the value of providing instruction. Still, when all is said and done, you have to decide if the instruction you have provided is ultimately worth the time, money, and effort devoted to it. Could all of the effort and resources you dedicated to a class have been put to better use on some other project or area of library operation? Even if the data suggest that the answer is no, that your instruction seems worthwhile, every librarian who provides instruction should frequently ask themselves if there are better ways to focus their efforts to improve the educational experience.

Suggestions

- Identify strengths and address weaknesses.
- Look ahead to the next assessment.
- Keep in mind that the hardest choices often produce the greatest rewards.
- Recognize that there may be several ways to address the same problem.

A FINAL WORD ON ASSESSMENT

Focus, focus, focus. Although noted earlier, it bears repeating that those conducting assessments need to be cautioned about trying to do too much with a single assessment. Focus is critical in facilitating data collection and producing meaningful, useful results. To that end, a single assessment should *not* be used to collect every possible piece of information about a particular class, concept, or instructional technique. Demographic data are useful in general, for example, but it is not necessary to collect data on, say, gender, unless you have a specific question about gender that such data might help answer. If the need or rationale for a specific assessment question is unclear, the data generated from it and their interpretation are likely to be unclear as well. For that reason alone, overassessing is often as bad as (or worse than) not assessing at all. Focusing on the reasons for doing the assessment in the first place makes for a much smoother assessment process from start to finish.

ELEVEN CHALLENGES TO INSTRUCTION

THERE ARE NUMEROUS CHALLENGES to any librarian who is considering providing instruction. Some of these challenges are practical, others more philosophical. They can limit the effectiveness of a class, the instruction librarian, or the library's overall instruction program. Some of the challenges instruction librarians are likely to face are very specific; many of them are discussed in earlier chapters. In any case, because their handling reflects on the librarian and library alike, all challenges need to be addressed in a positive, professional, and timely manner.

Many challenges are not easily placed within a specific category. This is particularly true for information literacy instruction and other attempts to embed information and research skills throughout the curriculum. Such endeavors can involve multiple departments, budgets, and priorities and therefore things over which the librarian has little or no control. As a result, addressing these challenges can often be particularly difficult and problematic.

FOUR COMMON MISCONCEPTIONS ABOUT LIBRARY INSTRUCTION

Despite radical changes to library resources and services in recent years, many stereotypes and misconceptions about libraries, librarians, and the research process still persist. Though not specifically challenges in and of themselves, these misconceptions can hinder the instruction process at any stage, from scheduling a class to providing the instruction itself. Instruction librarians need to work with classroom teachers and students to dispel or otherwise correct these misconceptions if instruction is to be successful.

Misconception 1: When Students Get to the Library, They Will Be Able to Figure Things Out

Many students are overwhelmed by the choices confronting them. Multiple formats and dozens (if not hundreds) of resources to choose from as well as an ever-growing array of access points to information are just the tip of the iceberg. Even if they know which resource to use and where to access it, many students often have no idea how to use the resource to find what they need. A variety of vendor interfaces and features, ever-changing resource lists, and new technologies emerging all of the time are just a few of the things that further exacerbate the situation.

Misconception 2: Students Know How to Do All "This Stuff"

With information's increasing dependence on computer technology, it is important to note that just because a student has some proficiency with a computer does not necessarily mean he can use those skills to locate and retrieve relevant information. Admittedly, many of today's students possess more computer skills than generations past and have a greater familiarity with a wider range of technologies. But that knowledge and those skills do not necessarily transfer to the effective and efficient use of information. Even tech-savvy students often are not aware of all of the library's resources, how to access them, or how to use them effectively.

Misconception 3: Students Have Previously Received Appropriate Instruction

Simply put, classroom instructors should not assume that a single instruction session is sufficient or that additional instruction is not needed. Lacking a universal and systematic approach to instruction, students' knowledge of information resources and the research process is often piecemeal. Unfortunately, classroom instructors often mistakenly believe that students have acquired all of the skills they need via another class. For example, many students are exposed to information resources and the research process as part of introductory classes such as English 101 or some sort of "First-Year Experience." Such classes, though, are not always mandatory or taught in the same way. Even if they are, these classes tend to be general and cannot possibly address the discipline-specific needs of upper-level courses. And because they are offered early in a student's career, what is taught may be forgotten if it is not reinforced and applied in subsequent courses and assignments.

Misconception 4: A Single Instruction Session Is Sufficient

Single-session classes are great for providing overviews and heightening awareness. But, just as a single class on organic chemistry cannot teach students everything there is to know about organic chemistry, no single class on the research process is sufficient either. What students learn, for example, may be applicable only to the particular class in which it was learned or for the assignment on which the instruction was based. What was taught may not have been clear, or students may not have understood how to apply that knowledge, particularly to other topics and assignments. Resources and features may have changed since the instruction was received. For these and other reasons, like anything, becoming effective researchers requires practice.

SPECIFIC CHALLENGES TO EFFECTIVE LIBRARY INSTRUCTION
Nonlibrarians Providing Instruction about Library Resources and Services

A growing number of nonlibrarians are providing their own instruction with respect to library and information skills and resources. In part, this may be attributed to the ubiquity and accessibility of the Internet and the growing number of library resources available remotely. Sometimes, though, classroom faculty members may have brought several classes to the library. As a result, they may feel completely at ease providing their own instruction. Either way, in this scenario the librarian is involved marginally, if at all, in developing or providing the instruction.

This scenario can be a mixed blessing. On the one hand, being a librarian does not necessarily mean knowing more about the resources the library has to offer or how to use them. It certainly does not imply that a librarian is better equipped to provide instruction. In fact, many classroom instructors are as (or more) knowledgeable about specific library resources and how to use them as librarians. Most arguably have significantly more teaching experience. In addition, their familiarity with the course's assignments and overall objectives enables them to provide an added level of relevance to their instruction that librarians often cannot.

With the above in mind, though, it needs to be noted that having nonlibrarians provide instruction is not without its drawbacks. For one, classroom instructors may not be up to date with the latest resources or how to use them effectively. Even though they may recently have attended an instruction session with their class, things change all the time. It is often difficult for librarians to keep up with the changes; it is even more so for those outside the library.

A related problem can occur with assignments. Because they are not involved with library resources on a daily basis, even the most well-intentioned instructors may be unaware of changes to resources, the way they are accessed, advanced resource search options, and so on. This can be particularly true of activities they might use or assign that they have found online or in a textbook. These templates may be too specific or too general to be of use locally. As a result, the instructor may be misspeaking or providing incorrect information, and librarians have to reeducate students about the correct or more effective way to do things.

The bottom line is that librarians need to acknowledge that they do not have a monopoly on either information or instruction. Characterizing library instruction as belonging to the library sets up an unnecessary barrier to true instruction and jeopardizes ongoing and future collaboration with classroom faculty. Similarly, librarians also need to recognize that they often cannot prevent nonlibrarians from providing instruction about library resources and services. Admittedly, removing the librarian from the equation risks marginalizing both the perceived and actual worth of librarians and libraries. However, if librarians use the time they would have spent on instruction to educate instructors about things such as new resources and features, they will develop greater rapport and generate an environment more conducive to greater overall use of the library.

Mental Models of Libraries and Librarians

Individuals' previous experience with libraries and librarians has a significant impact on how they perceive library instruction. Many instructors and students, for example, have difficulty accepting the notion of librarians as teachers. Prevailing stereotypes do nothing to dissuade this notion. This problem is further exacerbated by the fact that the work librarians do is often invisible or unclear; many people have difficulty distinguishing between librarians and other library staff members.

Concerns of Classroom Instructors

Although few would argue that library instruction is not beneficial, instruction librarians need to be aware that classroom instructors are faced with a growing number of practical considerations that can make requesting library instruction for their students a challenge. Fear of a loss of classroom time, budgetary concerns, and lack of assessment tools may also be behind some of the reluctance. In addition, there may be curricular constraints, accreditation needs, or other departmental or institutional issues that effectively limit teachers' windows of opportunity for including more library instruction than they already do.

When teachers face choices within their classroom and beyond, information literacy is often the loser. Although they may fully support the principles of information literacy, requiring it can be seen as an attack of sorts, since it implies that it should take precedence over other topics or concerns. It can also be seen as implying that research and information skills are not already being developed or that work that has been done is inadequate.

Lack of a Common Vocabulary

Lacking a common vocabulary, it is often difficult for librarians to discuss information literacy and generate support with faculty members. At its worst, because of the increasing interdependence of information and computer technology, some naively equate information literacy with computer literacy. Even those familiar with information literacy can be seen equating the idea with *lifelong learning, resource-based learning,* and *critical thinking.* Even among librarians—those generally seen as most familiar with it—information literacy may be seen as a replacement for or an extension or evolution of traditional instruction. As a result, even librarians use terms like *user education* and *bibliographic instruction* interchangeably with *information literacy instruction*.

Abstract Nature of Information Literacy

The fact that *information literacy* is an abstraction poses its own challenges. Although its various definitions have common elements and it is generally seen as being transferable to multiple environments, information literacy is not easily understood. Although it is easy to describe what makes an individual information-literate, it is hard to express exactly what that means. For example, is it an all-or-nothing concept, or are there degrees or levels of information literacy? If the competency standards adopted by the ACRL are the gauge, does someone have to master all five standards, or can they master three completely and the other two only partially and still be considered information literate? In short, is information literacy a set of skills to master or some sort of cognitive function? The abstract nature of the concept makes answering these questions difficult at best. In turn, meaningful assessment is particularly difficult because it is unclear how to identify individuals who have attained mastery if *mastery* is not defined.

Library Instruction Viewed as Library-Specific

Responsibility for library instruction—especially information literacy instruction—is often seen as a library responsibility, not a shared responsibility of everyone. Classes geared specifically to information literacy instruction further reinforce this perception. In turn, people come to perceive information literacy instruction as a separate discipline or field of study. Particularly when taught solely or primarily by librarians, information literacy can come to be seen in isolation from other topics or fields of study. Classroom faculty are often hesitant to take ownership because information literacy is seen as a library concern, not a concern for other disciplines.

DISRUPTIVE BEHAVIOR

Disruptive behavior poses its own unique set of challenges. Everyone who has taught has had to deal with disruptive behavior. Sometimes such behavior can be mild, such as when a student clicks away, updating her social networking profile as you are speaking about searching for articles. In other cases the disruption can be much more significant, such as yelling in class or threatening others. Mild or otherwise, all disruptions can be incredibly distracting to you and to the other students and can easily derail a class. Behaviors such as indifference, rudeness, threats, suggestive or otherwise inappropriate comments or behavior, and challenges to your authority or knowledge can be intimidating. Each of us handles such behaviors differently.

Whether in the classroom or as part of a feedback/assessment process, it is important for instructors to understand and be able to recognize the difference between comments and behaviors that are intended to be positive, constructive criticisms and those that are derogatory or intended to be personally hurtful. Suggestions about how to improve a class or presentation, for example, should always be welcomed. Even well-intentioned comments, though, can easily be misconstrued or misinterpreted. This can be especially true when the originator is verbally or behaviorally aggressive or when the person on the receiving end is defensive or insecure—personally or professionally.

To fully understand and properly interpret such comments, you need to understand them in the context from which they emerged. Unfortunately, this is not always as easy as it sounds. In most cases it is usually pretty clear from body language, word choices, and tone whether someone is providing criticism with the intent to help or to hurt. With the latter, it is important to recognize that the causes for such negativity may or may not have anything to do with the class, the instructor, or the instruction provided. For instance, sometimes people simply have bad days and, unfortunately, the instructor becomes the target of their frustration.

The bottom line? Do not take things personally. Experiencing some degree of negativity is unavoidable. It is part of being a teacher and happens to everyone at one time or another. Always keep in mind that rude, disruptive, or otherwise negative comments and behavior are generally the exception rather than the rule. And recognize that not every uncomfortable comment or behavior is an attack or meant to question an instructor's competence and abilities. Remain calm and professional, acknowledge the "good," use the "bad" to improve yourself—personally and professionally—and always move forward.

Suggestions

- Recognize the difference between being an authority and being authoritarian.
- Articulate your rules (and consequences) early and clearly.
- Do not try to change the student. Change how you respond.
- Employ classroom management software to control student behavior on workstations.

Librarianship is changing—in many and varied, often dramatic ways. But, at its core, librarianship remains a service profession. At the most fundamental level, librarians have always been and still are in the business of helping people. In the foreseeable future, this seems unlikely to change. What is changing, though, are the needs and expectations of today's information user. More than ever, there is a need for individuals to have adequate information skills.

To continue to convey relevance to today's library user, we librarians need to redefine ourselves and our profession. We can no longer simply view ourselves as passive providers of information. We need to take a more active role in the curricular process and become facilitators of learning. At the very least, this means recognizing that learning takes place outside the classroom, that every moment has the potential to be a teaching moment, and that all of us are teachers. More than that, though, it involves becoming more active participants in the learning process by serving as actual instructors and working with faculty to develop more meaningful assignments involving the library.

Information literacy holds great promise in this respect. There is still a need for and value in providing traditional forms of library instruction. At the same time, growing expectations from society in general and accrediting agencies in particular have resulted in a greater emphasis on information literacy and information literacy instruction. Because information literacy instruction requires a broad-based, multilevel, systematic, and comprehensive approach, librarians are well positioned to serve pivotal positions in this process. In so doing, librarians can reenergize themselves, their classes, and the profession as a whole. More important, librarians have an opportunity to become key leaders in preparing individuals to meet the needs of the information age.

INDEX